RUPTURED ATTACHMENT

THE HISTORICAL PROBLEM WITHIN
AFRICAN AMERICAN INTIMATE RELATIONSHIPS
AND WHY IT AFFECTS US TODAY

DR. SAMETTA HILL

authorHOUSE®

AuthorHouse™
1663 Liberty Drive
Bloomington, IN 47403
www.authorhouse.com
Phone: 1 (800) 839-8640

Published by AuthorHouse 02/27/2018

ISBN: 978-1-5462-3022-9 (sc)
ISBN: 978-1-5462-3021-2 (e)

Print information available on the last page.

Any people depicted in stock imagery provided by Getty Images are models, and such images are being used for illustrative purposes only. Certain stock imagery © Getty Images.

This book is printed on acid-free paper.

Contents

Dedication

To the black man who I have loved all my life. You are strong... you are Kings... you are loved and it is not your fault. To the black woman, you are valued... you are loved... you are beautiful inside and out, and it is not your fault. To my mother, Anna Scott, who gave me life and was a wonderful example of a strong, beautiful, encouraging courageous black woman. To my children who loved, supported and listened to me for many years to help turn this dream into a reality. To God for giving me this gift to share with the world in the hopes of bringing healing and restoration to this couple, family and group of people.

Acknowledgments

I would like to express sincere gratitude to my committee members, Dr. Joseph Genev-Reid and Dr. Brian D'Agostino for their invaluable support and guidance in the planning and implementation of this book. Gratefulness to Rozenia Fuller who gave me my first journal and said "You have a book in you." I am grateful for Dr. Bill Forisha who believed in me, challenged my thinking and encouraged me to write what was in my heart. I thank Dr. Phillip Valentine for providing insight and resources to help me articulate the black experience during the implementation of slaves in the United States. Gratefulness to Rakumba Gill who supported me, listened to me and comforted me through the process. I want to thank my children, my daughter Sametta who read my book to me; my son Qwalius who would research information, watched movies and documentaries with me; to my son X'Zarion who watched documentaries and challenged my thinking and asked questions about my project; my son Tarey, who is a strong black man, who provided Youtube clips for me to learn the history of the Moors. I appreciate all my family and friends who listened to me talk and process countless hours about this topic. Lastly, I want to give thankfulness to God for giving me wisdom, motivation and the courage to write this book.

Introduction

"Sealing off the past has been a way of dealing with the pain, hardship, humiliation, and degradation that have marked African American history from slave times to the presnt. But we are coming to realize that knowledge of the past, even if painful, can nourish a people's strength"

("Black genealogy revisited: Restorying an African American family," 2008, p. 114).

Research studies today account for relational problems of heterosexual African American heterosexual couples in terms of contemporary factors such as female headed households, mass incarceration, the racial achievement gap in academic performance, infidelity, etc. These contemporary explanations provide an incomplete understanding of the African American's experience in the United States. The contemporary explanation is surface and does not take into consideration the historical challenges of this group of people. Contemporary issues are a symptom not a basis for the issues the couples face today.

During slavery cruel physical and mental practices were used to gain social control and disrupt the intimate family structure and couple relationship. Psychological slavery is used, in this book, to describe the shift from physical bondage to mental bondage. After a period of time the slave owner no longer needed physical whips and chains to manage the intimate relationship between the African American man and woman; the practices of slavery and its transgenerational effects conditioned the mind of the African American and continues to have a mental hold that African American men women experience. Psychological slavery continues to contribute to the disruption of the family structure and couple relationship. "Only by exploring this painful history can we learn of the ingenious survival practices developed during and after slavery" (Black genealogy revisited: Restorying an African American family," 2008, p. 114).

My experience growing up in Des Moines, Iowa, as an African American person, caused me to question the social explanations provided as a reason these couples could not maintain their romantic relationship. Iowa felt like a very conservative state and Des Moines was very segregated. The relationship between whites and blacks was very conflictual. It seemed as though whites did not like us and we did not like them. The African American population was concentrated in one area. These three influences (conservative, segregated, relationship with whites) created a world that felt very racist. You could clearly see there was a divide. I never understood why we had this relationship with whites and when I asked family members they would simply say "they JUST don't like us." Nothing else was ever said… slavery and our slave experience was never talked about. From my vantage point, white couples and families were flourishing and in my community families and couples struggled to stay together. Social issues existed but those social issues did not seem to provide a full explanations of a root problem for African Americans specifically, for the African American family and more specifically the African American heterosexual couple. I often wondered what the history was for this couple and how did their way of being an African American couple develop? The relational problems the couples experienced seemed to be related to a historical issue that no one wanted to talk about.

Beginning in elementary school we were introduced to history. During history class we learned the history of many different groups and progressions people had made in history such as industrialization and feminism; the need for these progressions and why they came to be. We learned a lot about Native Americans and Asians; their cultures and traditions. We learned about slaves during slavery… the brutality endured; their role as laborers and working on plantations. I began to realize that slaves were African Americans who originated from Africa who now lived permanently in the United States. The information provided in history class was incomplete, it did not provide information regarding who we were before slavery; our culture and traditions, nor did it provide much information about who we were after slavery. This sparked my curiosity and I began to question who we are as a people, family and couple unit.

From a young age I began to watch African American couples interact and noticed a pattern of disconnect and lack of trust within the couple.

I could not understand why this problem existed and no one in my community was willing to talk about it. The couples I observed appeared to desire closeness and trust but those components appeared to be continually and considerably out of reach… something unseen seemed to get in the way of their ability to get close and trust one another. Closeness and trust felt obtainable but for some reason the mark was continually missed. It was almost as if this couple did not know the skills or were afraid to build the closeness and trust they seemed to desire.

I have always been *"In Love with the Black man"* and even in my own life I have experienced my own difficulty and inability to get close and trust in an intimate relationship with a black man. I also felt as though he had trouble with me in regards to closeness and trust. Despite my diligent efforts to learn how to obtain closeness and trust I continued to experience lack of trust and disconnect for the black man I have been in love with since childhood. My fruitless efforts of therapy (individual and couple), church, self-help books, conversations with men etc. have not gotten me any closer to the root of this issue. More importantly, I have yet to obtain the closeness and trust I would like to have in this relationship. In the avenues I pursued to try to resolve the issue (therapy, church self-help books etc.) the historical experience of the implementation of slavery and the process of making slaves was never part of the conversation. What I learned from history is that people evolved to survive the changes of the world and to progress themselves in the world. This couples evolution allowed them to survive and progress at the loss of closeness and trust within the intimate relationship.

I believe the contemporary issues used to explain the problems between the couple are symptoms due to an historical systematic implementation and process of making slaves. The contemporary explanation for the issues do not take into consideration the historical challenges this group had to endure. The systematic implementation and process of making slaves had a profound adverse impact on the couple by nullifying the relationship.

This book will provide clinicians and all readers with insight regarding the historical problem impacting this intimate couple relationship. In addition, the book will highlight the relational issues this couple experiences as it pertains to attachment, trust, and intimacy.

The book will begin with a description of the family viewed from the Functionalist Perspective to explain the importance of the family structure and pertinent roles for the couple; a discussion of the contemporary issues and the social explanations viewed under functionalist theory and intimacy; special attention will be given to foundational issues involving attachment and trust in relationships using Attachment theory (having delineated the historical traumas and their contemporary manifestations and a description of the attachment rupture that occurred during the implementation and process of slavery and the attachment style inherited by this group); finally, a recommendation for treating couples to assist in understanding and repairing the historical attachment rupture.

For the purpose of this book *Trust* is defined from the functionalist perspective. *Trust* is defined for women: the woman will be able to receive protection from men and economic support. *Trust* is defined for men: the man will be able to receive emotional support from the woman. During the implantation and process of slavery these two relational components were intentionally abolished.

Intimate defines the relationship between the couple that involves physical or emotional intimacy, a romantic attachment that may or may not include sexual activity.

The Functionalist Perspective

Role of the family

According to Functionalist Theory (Parsons & Bales, 1955), the family is the most important social institution. Through this institution, children establish emotional ties and begin to internalize such things as cultural norms and values. Family—the association of individuals by ancestry, marriage or adoption--provides stability. Functionalism's core concepts provide an understanding of the family's role in helping children to develop and become productive in society. According to Parsons & Bales (1955) the best structure for socializing children and stabilizing adult personality to meet the needs of others and of society is the intact family (p. 16). They examine how the family develops its members and assigns roles in a way that meshes with the economic needs of society (Parsons and Bales, p.19). Although family has taken many different forms, it continues to perform these core functions. If this were not true, functionalist theory holds, the family would have been selected out and replaced by other structures (Parsons & Bales, 1955). Functionalism considers the intact family to be the best structure for socializing and developing its members and views any deviation from this structure (i. e. single-parent families) as not serving its members well.

Socialization of Children

The family has two central functions: the socialization of children and stabilization of adult personality (Parsons & Bales, 1955). Socialization of children occurs in the early stages of childhood, when the child's personality is shaped to encompass the core values of the society in which the family is immersed. Through this process, a society's core values become an integral part of the child (Parsons & Bales, 1955, p. 18). Children are born without any culture; they acquire it from their parents in the family, both through the explicit verbal instruction they receive and what they infer from observing parents as they enact the roles allotted to them by society.

Parsons & Bales (1955) state, "The human personality is not 'born' but must be 'made' through the socialization process that in the first instance families are necessary" (p. 16). Through socialization in the family, girls learn the roles of daughter, friend, sister, wife and mother. In addition, by observing the roles that family members play in society, children learn about socioeconomic structures and societal expectations associated with occupational roles (Parsons & Bales, 1955). Thus, it is through the family and the attitudes and cultural values imparted explicitly and implicitly during child rearing that society shapes the emerging personality of children in the most profound possible ways (Parsons & Bales, 1955). The intact family was dismantled during slavery; African culture, expected roles and traditions were not imparted in children during that time. Socialization of children occurred with the intentional absence of African custom.

Stabilization of Adult Personality

The stabilization of adult personality occurs in a marriage where the couple has emotional security (Parsons & Bales, 1955). Parsons and Bales (1955) describe the ideal family structure as the nuclear family, a marriage between a man and a woman with children (p. 11). Traditionally, marriage was viewed as a mutually beneficial exchange between a man and a woman. Through marriage, a woman could receive protection from men and economic support. Men received emotional support, sexual support, household maintenance and the reproduction of members (children).

This book does not endorse the sex stereotyping and heterosexual assumptions about marriage and family embedded in Parsons' and Bales' work. This limitation is not germane to my book, which focuses on the historical and transgenerational impacts of slavery on traditional heterosexual marriages. Notwithstanding the limitations of Parsons and Bales in other contexts, for my purposes, their conceptual framework continues be profoundly relevant.

According to Functionalist Theory, the family regulates sexual activity and provides physical care as well as psychological and emotional security to its members (Parsons & Bales, 1955). The family allows adults to act out playful dimensions of their personality by engaging their children through play. According to Parsons & Bales (1955), men and women have distinct roles in the family (p. 20). Women provide affection, care, love, security and all of the needed emotional support, which the authors designate as the "expressive role" (p. 23). The man's role in the family—that of sole provider—is "instrumental." This role is strenuous and carries with it a lot of challenges to the point a man could break down. The woman's function is to provide love and understanding so that he can continue to carry out his function on behalf of the family. The successful functioning of the family thus depends on men and women carrying out these "expressive" and "instrumental" roles assigned to them by society (Parsons & Bales, 1955). The organization and assignment of differentiated role tasks, in addition to serving the family's survival, provides a setting in which the interpersonal relationships and mutual understanding of its members can develop. During the implementation of slavery the ideal family structure was dismantled and the instrumental and expressive roles were transposed. Woman were no longer able to provide affection, care, love and security for their partner. The emotional support the woman once gave to her partner was not allowed. Men were reduced to breeders. They were no longer able to provide and protect their family. This basic function was stripped and caused a great disconnect for this couple.

Parental roles in the family help to develop a secure attachment in the child. This attachment style will be the one the child carries into his adult life. The childhood experience with his parents is what he will expect in future relationships with others; more specifically in a romantic relationship with someone.

Neo-Functionalism brings together the two concepts of functionalism and attachment theory to provide greater understanding of the foundational problems this couple continues to experience today due to the lack of attachment they were not allowed to experience during the implementation of slavery.

NeoFunctionalism

Neo-Functionalism was developed by Don Swenson, who in 2004 had an interest in uniting the diverse family theoretical frameworks through the lens of functionalism. He adopts the functionalist concept that families meet the needs of the social system and of individuals (Swenson, 2004). Building on and going beyond classical functionalism, Swenson also adopts attachment theory from psychology to create a unified, empirically based family theory. Neo-functionalism explains how the family meets the developmental needs of children and develops their emotional, cognitive and behavioral skills.

After summarizing the traditional functionalist theory developed by Talcott Parsons, Swenson examines its pervasive influence to varying degrees on a wide range of family theories. On this basis, he develops a unified theory of the family system. Going beyond Parsons' focus on function, Swenson chose to emphasize the attachment style between mother and child (Swenson, 2004). He retained Parsons' view that an intact family provides the optimum structure for development of the child and stabilization of adult personality. From the viewpoint of attachment theory, the regular interaction and interdependence provided by the family are salient. Swenson (2004) holds that parental roles (expressive and instrumental) and parental tasks are necessary for the child's secure attachment and socialization (p. 263). Following attachment theory in psychology, he notes that in families with negative parenting, children develop insecure attachment. This, in turn, leads to behavioral issues and substandard learning performance. Such children do not integrate into society well, nor meet the needs of society (Swenson, 2004).

While Parson's functionalism was rooted in Freudian psychoanalysis, Swenson's neofunctionalism is rooted in Attachment Theory, which is more empirically based (Swenson, 2004). Swenson also thinks it is important to examine all forms of the family, not just the intact heterosexual family (Swenson, 2004), though he believes along with Parsons that alternative family structures create less secure attachment and negative outcomes for children, including defiance and nonconformity. Parson and Swenson both emphasize stability, and associate change with deviance and nonconformity, which they consider pathological (Swenson, 2004), even though change is a natural part of the human experience.

The structure of slavery and its practices was not a conducive environment to develop securely attached children who would grow to be adults who would develop healthy intimate relationships and integrate into society well. Neo-functionalism explains that it is the intact family, the attachment between the mother and child and the interaction and interdependency that allows the child to develop a secure attachment that will carry over into their adult relationships.

Social explanations have been provided to explain the breakdown of this couple. Contemporary explanations are useful but provides an incomplete understanding. Contemporary issues are a symptom not a basis for the issues these couples face today. The next chapter will provide these contemporary views. The contemporary explanations will be explored through functionalist theory to highlight the deviation from the ideal family and the consequences of that deviation. Family, tradition, culture and roles were a part of the fabric of African culture prior to slavery but were abolished by slavery. Systematic institutions (i.e. welfare) were implemented to keep the family dismantled and the couple disconnected.

Contemporary Issues

Most of the available psychological research on the relational problems of heterosexual African American couples attributes the breakdown in families and the heterosexual couple to contemporary factors such as female headed households, mass incarceration, the racial achievement gap in academic performance, and infidelity. According to Functionalist theory these factors impact the organization and assignment of differentiated role tasks, in addition to serving the family's survival, provides a setting in which the interpersonal relationships and mutual understanding of its members are unable to develop. The contemporary issues provide a surface explanation but are not the basis for the issues this couple face today. The explanation does not take into account the historical challenge this couple had to endure. The contemporary explanation does not provide the full interpretation of the issues with intimacy and trust. I contend that the contemporary explanations are the symptoms of a historical rupture that occurred during the implementation and process of slavery.

In the United States, African American households are more frequently headed by females than White and Hispanic households. Vespa, Lewis, and Kreider (2013) provide a current description of the family composition and households in the United States (p. 1). They report, "Black children (55 percent) and Hispanic children (31 percent) were more likely to live with one parent than non-Hispanic White children (21 percent) and Asian children (13 percent)" (p. 2). Families with children under age 18 it was more common for African American families to have only a mother than for Whites, Hispanics and Asians. Specifically, "Blacks had the highest percentage of mother-only family groups and householders and living with other relatives (29 percent and 22 percent, respectively), followed by Hispanics (18 percent and 14 percent). The percentage of mother-only with children under age 18 for White mothers is 9.6 percent followed by Asians at 5.7 percent." (Vespa, Lewis, and Kreider, 2013). The optimal environment for the socialization of children and stabilization of adult personality is an intact family. A mother and father carrying out their instrumental and expressive roles in the family. According to this report the black father is missing from this home. This means that the family is missing the economic provision and protection of this member. Male children are not observing and learning to be instrumental members in these families and the females are not able to observe and learn how a man carries out this role. In addition, the male and female children are not able to observe and learn how the mother provides affection, care, love, security and all of the needed emotional support for the father of this household. The absence of the father in these homes impacts the socialization and stabilization of the adult personality for these members.

High incarceration rates are another issue identified as a cause of stress and breakup of the Black family. It has been reported that the group with the highest incarceration rate is African American men. "An estimated 516,900 black males were in state or federal prison at yearend 2014, accounting for 37% of the male prison population. White males made up 32% of the male population (453,500 prison inmates), followed by Hispanics (308,700 inmates or 22%)" (Carson, 2014). With so many black men incarcerated we again begin to see the deviation from the ideal family makeup according to the functionalist perspective. The instrumental role is missing from these households with children. This father is not able to protect and provide for his family and the children are not able to observe and learn the instrumental role he is responsible to carry out. The mother in this family is not able to demonstrate love, care, security and all emotional needs for this man in front of the children so that they have a template, a frame of reference for their families.

It has also been supported by numerous studies that African Americans score significantly lower than Whites on various measures of academic achievement. The academic achievement gap is not only an educational problem but also a socioeconomic problem for African American men and women (Leach & Williams, 2007). High school completion rates among persons 18-24 years of age in 2001 were 91.8% for Whites and 83.7% for African Americans (Kaufman et. al., 2001). According to Leach and Williams (2007) "The persistence of the academic achievement gap has long-term effects beyond college (p. 48). The socioeconomic effect the African American experiences is due to the achievement gap and has a generational impact on African American children and families. Higher education provides adults access to an increase in earning potential.

The academic achievement gap is particularly consequential for Blacks considering the racial disparity in earnings for Blacks and Whites with the same level of education. Over a life span, Whites' work-life earnings without a high school diploma is $1.1 million, whereas, African American work-life earnings is 0.8 Million (Day & Newburger, 2002). The academic achievement gap thus compounds and amplifies Black-White socioeconomic inequality and is a contributing factor to adverse social conditions such as poverty, discrimination, social disadvantage and institutional barriers (Leach & Williams, 2007). These adverse social conditions undoubtedly put a strain on the intimate relationships of African American couples. For many Black families the result is applying to a government program which impacts the family by rewarding women with assistance (cash, food stamps housing etc.) if there is no father in the home. These systemic institutional systems create barriers for the instrumental and expressive roles for these black men and women. Lack of education for the black man results in his inability to take care of his family. In many cases some black men have resorted to illegal activity to support their families which in turn results in them being incarcerated and separated from their family. Leaving them with little to no protection and no economic support. Incarceration puts an emotional strain on the relationship and results in the woman not being able to provide the emotional support recommended by the functionalist perspective.

Finally, infidelity may also be a social issue that impacts the heterosexual African American couple's ability to stay together. According to Treas and Giesen (2000a), African Americans are more likely than any other race to engage in infidelity and the authors cite studies suggesting that African American men are more likely than men of others races to engage in infidelity (p. 224). The way the study reads one may believe that black men engage in infidelity for sport. The history of slavery provides an explanation for this behavior. Black men during slavery were forced to be breeders. This is not a role or function outlined in the functionalist perspective. Functionalist theory states that the family regulates sexual activity. The family is where a boy learns to be a man, brother, uncle, husband etc. The sexual practices and regulations in slavery taught these men to be breeders. They stripped away their right to be in an intimate relationship with a black woman. Thus socializing these men as breeders may be a direct generational transmission of behavior we continue to see in black men today.

This book does not dispute the importance of female headed households, mass incarceration, the racial achievement gap in academic performance, infidelity, and other contemporary factors shaping Black family and intimate life. These very factors and the relationship problems to which they contribute do not exist in an historical vacuum and cannot be adequately understood apart from ongoing intergenerational trauma associated with slavery (Graff, 2014). The present book aims to examine this neglected psycho-historical dimension of contemporary African American intimate relationships, with intentional attention to the foundational disruption of attachment, trust stemming from the experience of slavery and its intergenerational traumatic effects. Beyond contemporary issues I wish to aid in the understanding of the African experience. Through the use of the Functionalist theory the following chapters will describe family life in Africa, its culture and traditions, which align with the functionalist perspective. As well as a description of the slave family that was shaped in the United States due to the implementation of slavery. The goal in presenting the information is to illustrate that the original African family mirrored the intact family described in Functionalist Theory. Contemporary issues says that we did not have these values; information provided will clearly show that African families carried out instrumental and expressive roles according to their culture.

The African Family

Every culture has its own rules regarding roles and its own way of socializing children. While the content of cultures vary, adults everywhere and at all times teach the next generation the particular rules and roles that are expected in their society. The family stabilizes the adult personality and provides emotional support. Every culture has its own view of what that might look like. Pre-slavery healthy adults in Africa were expected to marry and carry out distinct roles within their family. Prior to the transport of enslaved Africans to the New World, family life was patterned according to descent, type of marriage, type of family, inhabited area, child care and protection (Billingsley, 1968). Marriage and structure were valued and widely ingrained in the culture. In West Africa, there were three forms of marriage: monogamy, polyandry and polygyny (Billingsley, 1968). "Of the three basic forms of marriage, monogamy, which unites one man and one woman, was the most common throughout West Africa, from where American Negroes came" (Billingsley, 1968, p. 42). Contrary to popular belief, prior to slavery African people believed in and valued monogamy in the marriage.

Billingsley (1968) described pre-slavery African society as follows:

> *"First, family life was not primarily—or even essentially–the affair of two people who happened to be married to each other. It united not simply two people, but two families with a network of extended kin who had considerable influence on the family, and considerable responsibility for its development and well-being. Marriage could neither be entered into nor abandoned without substantial community support. Secondly, marriage and family life in pre-European Africa, as among most tribal people, was enmeshed in centuries of tradition, ritual, custom, and law" (p. 39).*

Olaudah Equiano or Gustavus Vassa, *The African* explains that in Africa Adultery was punished with slavery or death. Monogamy was an expectation in Africa and the practice of punishment with slavery or death was widely practiced.

Socialization of children

The role and responsibility of African fathers was to raise children into moral, civic and economically responsible adults (Billingsley, 1968). "The father played a very important role in the care and protection of the children in all these West African societies" (Billingsley, 1968, p. 43). Pre-slavery, the mother-child relationship was also vital; mother and child were expected to be inseparable until the child was weaned at age one or two (Billingsley, 1968).

Fortes (2008) asserts that strong attachment of both male and female children to the mother carries over into adulthood:

> *"Ashanti say that throughout her life, a woman's foremost attachment is to her mother, who will always protect and help her. A woman grows up in daily and unbroken intimacy with her mother, learns all feminine skills from her, and above all, derives her character from her… For a man, his mother is his most trusted confidante, especially in intimate personal matters. A man's first ambition is to gain enough money to be able to build a house for his mother if she does not own one. To be mistress of her own home, with her children and daughters' children around her, is the highest dignity an ordinary woman aspires to"* (p. 263).

Pre-slavery the social expectation was for men and women to marry and have children and raise them according to long-standing traditions, beliefs and values. Through the roles carried out in this culture, girls learned to be daughters, friends and sisters. In the same respect, boys learned the socially expected occupational roles by observing their fathers.

Stabilization of adult personality

The African cultural belief was generally that marriage helps the man and the woman to be healthy and provides emotional security. Billingsley (1968) explains "The most striking feature of African family and community life was the strong and dominate place in family and society assigned to and assumed by the men. This strong, masculine dominance, however, far from being capricious authoritarianism, was supported, guided, and limited by custom and tradition, which also provided a substantial role for the women" (p. 40). The African family mimics the functionalist perspective as most African men were married to one woman. The men were in instrumental roles, they provided economic support and protection for their wife and children (Billingsley, 1968). The women were in expressive roles and provided emotional support to their husbands and children as well as household maintenance, the reproduction of members (children), and sexual support for their husbands (Parsons & Bales, 1955).

The implementation and process of slavery dismantled the African family structure and the roles within the family. Men and women were no longer able to carry out the instrumental and expressive roles from their native land. This can only be understood by a description of the Slave family.

The Slave Family

As reported by Billingsley (1968) "Negros were forcibly uprooted from a long history of strong family and community life every bit as viable as that of their captors" (p. 39). In slavery, the intentional disruption of the family totally disrupted the traditional family structure, including the socialization of children and stabilization of adult personality. Bennett (1969) declares "Slavery was a black man who stepped out of his hut {in West Africa} for a breath of fresh air and ended up ten months later in Georgia with bruises on his back and a brand on his chest" (p. 30-31). Through this process, Africans became progressively and forcibly more disengaged from their cultures, families, and their own humanity (Bennett 1969).

During the history of slavery in the United States, the term "Slave Family" was used but was an oxymoron since there was no such structure as the term "family" is normally understood. African people were brought over from Africa to the Americas either as isolated individuals or as families that were quickly, universally, and routinely dismantled. This practice served to ensure that the slaves would not bond, come together and revolt against the cruelty and abuse they were experiencing in the United States.

First Negro family in the united states

The origin of the Negro family in America was that of Anthony and Isabella, who were among the original twenty Negroes brought to Jamestown in 1619, one year before the Mayflower. This married couple had a son William in 1624, "the first Negro child born in English America" (Bennet, 1969). These first twenty Negroes who were brought to the Americas were treated like indentured servants. Beginning around 1690, most Negroes brought to America were captured in Africa and sold as slaves. They came from a long history of respected traditional African family life but were subjected to an immense "social and psychological disruption" (Billingsley, 1968).

This virtually complete cutoff destabilized the Negro family in America, destroying the traditional African social structure. Billingsley (1968) notes:

> *"First, moving as they did from Africa to the New World, the Negroes were confronted with an alien culture of European genesis. Thus, unlike some of the later migrants, including the Germans, Irish, and Italians, they were not moving into a society in which the historical norms and values and ways of life were familiar and acceptable. Secondly, they came from many different tribes with different languages, cultures, and traditions. Thirdly, they came without their families and often without females at all. In the fourth place, they came in chains" (p. 49).*

The adaptation of these Negroes to the European colonial culture prevailing in America was impeded because they were not allowed to keep their African families intact. Donoghue (2008) asserts:

> *"Further, from a functionalist perspective, servitude failed to provide a number of prerequisites for the family to function. The universal components included regulation of sexual conduct, replacement of members from generation to generation through reproduction, the socialization required so that children could develop emotional, cognitive and behavioral skills. Not to mention the provision by the family of an environment in which basic needs such as warmth, food, shelter and care could be met" (p. 251).*

Across all cultures, we generally find self-reinforcing social structures. Not so with the slave family, the conditions of which completely destabilized the ideal family structure described by functionalism.

In the book *"Life of Josiah Henson,"* Josiah (a slave) provides a description of what family living quarters were like during that time.

> *"Our lodging was in log huts, of a single small room, with no other floor than the trodden earth, in which ten or*

a dozen persons – men, women, and children – might sleep, but which could not protect them from dampness and cold, nor permit the existence of the common decencies of life. There were neither beds, nor furniture of any description – a blanket being the only addition to the dress of the day for protection from the chilliness of the air or the earth" (p. 6-7).

There is nothing in this description corresponding to what we normally understand as a family home in the United States. Displaced and isolated individuals have been thrown together in a common physical space, which is far from a husband, wife and their children with possibly some extended family living under one roof. Josiah describes a place where persons who are considered to be less than human reside in deplorable conditions, with little provision for dignity, warmth or protection. Contrast this with Parsons' and Bales' (1955) description of the American family:

"This "isolation" is manifested in the fact that the members of the nuclear family, consisting of parents and their still dependent children, ordinarily occupy a separate dwelling not shared with members of the family of orientation of either spouse, and that this household is in the typical case economically independent, subsisting in the first instance from the occupational earnings of the husband-father" (p.10).

Sojourner Truth describes the accommodations provided by her master Charles Ardinburgh. He had built a hotel and assigned the cellar under the hotel as the sleeping apartment for the slaves.

"… all the slaves he possessed, of both sexes, sleeping (as is quite common in a state of slavery) in the same room… Its only lights consisting of a few panes of glass, through which she thinks the sun never shone, but with thrice reflected rays; and the space between the loose boards of the floor, and the uneven earth below, was often filled with mud and water, the uncomfortable splashings of which were as annoying as its noxious vapors must have been chilling and fatal to

health. She shudders, even now, as she goes back in memory, and revisits the cellar, and sees its inmates, of both sexes and all ages, sleeping on those damp boards, like the horse, with little straw and a blanket; and she wonders not at the rheumatisms, and fever-sores, and palsies, that distorted the limbs and racked the bodies of those fellow-slaves in after-life" (Andrews & Gates, 2002, p. 576).

The conditions of life recounted by the slave Josiah bear little resemblance to this description of family by Parsons and Bales.

Socialization of children

Under slavery in colonial America and the United States, parents were prohibited from socializing their own children, a role that was taken over by the slave owner. Harriet Ann Jacobs a former slaved described slave-children as children without a father or mother (Andrews & Gates, 2002). Most children experienced broken bonds and no daily interaction with their parents (Dunaway, 2003). Slave owners controlled the rearing of slave children and family bonds were an obstacle to their primary goal, which was to create laborers as soon as possible who be entirely dependent on the master. On workdays, slave children received little or no supervision from their parents, who had to spend their entire workday in the fields or other plantation workplaces. Children were kept in plantation nurseries with their peers from other slave families, where they typically experienced malnutrition and injury due to poor supervision.

Such arrangements demolished the bond between slave parents and their children. Dunaway states,

"On the one hand, masters, not mothers, made fundamental decisions about the nature of child care: when, where, by whom, how much or how little. On the other hand, enslaved mothers did not have the option of not reporting to work when their children needed attention. Mothers risked punishment of children if they demanded better child care when the master's arrangements endangered their offspring.

> *If the mother's caregiving conflicted with the master's work,
> she was required to do her "productive" work, most often in
> the fields or at the nonagricultural sites" (p. 69-70).*

The slave owner did not benefit economically from slaves bonding with their family but purposely isolated the slave children from their families and made them entirely dependent on the slave owner. Children were brought at a higher price on the market if they were sold separate from their family. Henry Bibb, a former slave, describes his experience of being separated from his mom and forced into slave labor.

> *"The first time I was separated from my mother, I was young and small. I knew nothing of my condition then as a slave. I was living with Mr. White, whose wife died and left him a widower with one little girl, who was said to be the legitimate owner of my mother, and all her children. This girl was also my playmate when we were children.*
>
> *I was taken away from my mother, and hired out to labor for various persons, eight or ten years in succession; and all my wages were expended for the education of Harriet White, my playmate" (Andrews & Gates, 2002, p.441-442).*

Slavery interrupted the disciplinary role between parents and their children. Viewing both slave parents and children as his property, the slave owner believed it was his prerogative to exercise parental authority over the children (Dunaway, 2003). Dunaway asserts that "Nearly three-fifths of the Appalachian ex-slaves identified the white masters, mistress or children as the individuals who administered verbal or physical punishment to them most often. In this way, slaveholders undermined the authority of slave parents" (p. 75). The desired result of discipline was to teach children to obey the rules and work to prevent punishment or sale by the slave owner.

Lastly, slave children were socialized to begin working around five or six years old, at which age they were put under the supervision of overseers during the work day. Children who had been together in the plantation nursery were split up and assigned to do chores in the fields, the slave owner's home, or other sites. "A majority of Appalachian slaves experienced lost childhoods in which they were pressured to grow up fast and to take care of themselves. Mothers attenuated child rearing because their sons and daughters were put to work at an early age". These children never experienced playtime in a safe space and in the service of their own development. They went from the trauma of separation from their parents, to neglect in the plantation nursery, to the further trauma of separation from their childhood peers and enlistment into the harsh world of regimented, forced labor, which was their whole life's purpose under the system of slavery (Dunaway, 2003).

Stabilization of adult personality

As destabilizing as the above practices were for the slave family, when its individual members lived and worked on the same estate, the family structure could persist in some form, however broken. Even worse, the buying, selling, and trading of slaves often dismantled families altogether and dispersed their individual members to different localities. These separations completely deprived adults of the family's stabilizing effects on personality and transmitted traumatic effects across many generations into the present (Billingsley, 1968, p. 51; Graff, 2014). One out of four slave marriages was disrupted immediately upon slave owners relocating slaves, selling slaves, giving slaves to their children, or hiring out slaves as laborers (Dunaway, 2003)

This dismantling of families kept the Africans from bonding and rising up against the cruelties they were experiencing. Separating families was a way to defeat the protective attitudes that their members naturally develop toward one another. This enabled white slave masters to maintain social control and avoid uprisings that could cost them their wealth. A slave family that was not completely destroyed by the buying, selling, or lynching of its individual members was still subject to extremely long work days and other stresses that made normal family life impossible.

Donoghue (2008) states "The creation of the new Negro involved the inculcation of new sexual norms, a contrived family unit, a division of labor dictating that women played triple and often contradictory roles, as vehicles of procreation, propagation and reproduction" (p.168). Slave masters understood the dynamics of family structure and its empowering effects on its members. To maintain control and a productive slave economy, they routinely undermined family structure in all the ways indicated above and in many cases completely dismantled families. Harriet Ann Jacobs, a former slave, gives an account of a practice called Hiring-day that took place on New Year's Day:

> *"On one of these sale days, I saw a mother lead seven children to the auction-block. She knew that some of them would be taken from her; but they took all. The children were sold to a slave-trader, and their mother was bought by a man in her own town. Before night her children were all far away. She begged the trader to tell her where he intended to take them; this he refused to do. How could he, when he knew he would sell them, one by one, wherever he could command the highest price? I met that mother in the street, and her wild, haggard face lives to-day in my mind. She wrung her hands in anguish, and exclaimed, "Gone! All gone! Why don't God kill me?" I had no words wherewith to comfort her. Instances of this kind are of daily, yea, of hourly occurrence" (Andrews & Gates, 2002, p. 761-762).*

History provides evidence of a shift that moves from a focus on dismantling the family to rupturing the attachment between the African American couple. A review of the Willie Lynch letter will provide insight into the process by which the rupture between the couple was able to be accomplished.

Willie Lynch

Willie Lynch Letter

> *-Frederick Douglas-*
> *"Mr. Severe was rightly named: he was a cruel man. I have seen him whip a woman, causing the blood to run half an hour at the time; and this, too, in the midst of her crying children, pleading for their mother's release. He seemed to take pleasure in manifesting his fiendish barbarity"* (Andrews *& Gates, 2002, p. 288).*

The Willie Lynch Letter has been in print since at least 1970, but first received wide notice in the 1990s, when it appeared on the Internet. The Willie Lynch letter has not been proven to have historical premise nor has the letter been affirmed by an historian to be an historic reality cemented into history. This letter may not be a true document, however this letter appears to contain practices that may have been implemented during slavery. Unfortunately, we do not have any historians who have examined and provided a written account of the process for making slaves during this period. Historians have not researched this area to validate all the practices that went on, however, we do have slave narratives, stories have been passed down and documentaries created to provide a window of knowledge to the experience. Bartolome de las Casas was a 16th century historian who wrote about the cruel practices of the Spaniards against the Native Americans they enslaved. These practices were documented in the book *"The Tears of the Indians"*; this book, written by an historian, has been used as evidence of the similar practices African people experienced from white slave owners in the United States.

In addition, the Willie Lynch letter became highly recognized in the black community at the Million Man March (held in Washington, DC) on October 16th, 1995, When Minister Louise Farrakhan included it in his speech. He stated:

> *"We, as a people who have been fractured, divided and destroyed because of our division, now must move toward*

a perfect union. Let's look at a speech, delivered by a white slaveholder on the banks of the James River in 1712…. Listen to what he said. He said, 'In my bag, I have a foolproof method of controlling Black slaves. I guarantee every one of you, if installed correctly, it will control the slaves for at least 300 years'… So spoke Willie Lynch 283 years ago".

Since then, the letter has often been promoted as an authentic account of how slaves were created and conditioned during the 18th century. There are those who have pointed out inaccuracies and anachronisms that have led historians to conclude that the letter is fraudulent. Regardless of the veracity of the Willie Lynch letter, in this one letter someone articulated the practices that we historically know were implemented. The African American deplorable slave experience is purposely left out of American history and is hidden from African American people. After the freeing of slaves in 1865 until today, many African Americans were not allowed to talk about what happened during slavery, nor ask questions to their grandparents or great grandparents about the experience. Many elders in the African American community felt a lot of shame about the experience and chose not to speak of it again. It is also true that the United States has a lot of control over the media and has denied African Americans access to information about their history during slavery and prior to slavery, as a way to discount the atrocities this group has experienced.

In 1995 a speech surfaced, on the internet that claimed in 1712, Willie Lynch delivered a speech to other slaveholders about how to make slaves. In 1712, it was claimed that, Willie Lynch wrote an infamous letter outlining what he claimed was a full-proof method of indoctrinating and controlling black slaves:

"Let us make a slave. What do we need? First of all we need a black nigger man, a pregnant nigger woman and her baby nigger boy. Second, we will use the same basic principle that we use in breaking a horse, combined with some more sustaining factors. What we do with horses is that we break them from one form of life to another that is we reduce them from their natural state in nature. Whereas nature provides

> *them with a natural capacity to take care of their offspring,
> we break that natural string of independence from them and
> thereby create a dependency status, so that we may be able to
> get from them useful production for our business and pleasure
> (Lynch, 1712)."*

During slavery, it was an intentional practice to break up family members to disrupt all functions and bonding ingrained by the family. By breaking up the family, the protective nature of the family was destroyed. According to Dunaway (2003),

> *"The breakup of a marriage had a "geometric" impact
> upon the slaves involved. It directly affected a particular
> husband and wife, their children, their parents, and other
> kin nearby. It was also known to slave neighbors and to those
> who came to know the partners after union's dissolution. Such
> awareness spread over space following sale, but when children
> were involved, it also moved forward in time"* (p. 83).

Those who implemented the practices in the Willie Lynch letter had a basic understanding of the function of the family and the importance of the family structure for socializing children and stabilizing the adult personality. The persons who implemented this practice needed to disrupt the family function so that slaves were unable to keep their ties to their family. By attacking the family structure and function the slave family would not be able to maintain their bond and loyalty to one another thus keep intact the natural function to protect the family and rebel. The family staying intact and connected to their traditions, values and beliefs was detrimental to the white slave owner who needed to have fear and control over his property. He needed the bond between the members, specifically between the husband and wife to be broken, so that the bond would become weaker and weaker with the from generation to generation and each generation would be conditioned and taught by the previous generation to obey the white master and take on his societal norms. Slaves were not considered human, therefore, the importance of keeping the family structure was not important for the social development of the children and their ability to function in society. The goal was not for slaves to function as a family structure but independently for good economy.

Individuals today are still intrigued by the Willie Lynch letter and continue to have conversations, write books, and create movies about these methods and the intergenerational trauma associated with them. Alvin Morrow wrote the book "Breaking the Curse of Willie Lynch" to provide his perspective of how and why the historical practice identified in the Lynch letter continues to affect the relationship between the African American man and woman; which consequently has lingering effects for the African American family. He believed that Willie Lynch understood the function of the family; the roles of the husband and wife in that structure; the power differential in the roles and what that power balance meant for the healthy functioning for the couple to develop attachment and trust. Due to this reversal of the instrumental and expressive roles and the division in the relationship Morrow (2003) asserts:

> *"In the process of dividing the black male and the female, the objective of control became easier due to the fact that the slave makers only have a half of a people to manage. This is the reason for the manipulation of differences. Because once you split a peoples commonly shared ideal, you can divide the individuals even further by injecting a foreign concept as a solution once they have been split apart"* (p.28-29).

Here is how the practices described in the Willie Lynch Letter attacked the socialization and stabilization through the repositioning of roles that took place during the making of slaves. What is implied is that the instrumental role and expressive role was repositioned for the slave couple. The woman was repositioned in the instrumental role. The slave master was able to negotiate with her, she was able to provide in some ways for her children and protect them by adhering to the slave master's demands. The man was repositioned in the expressive role. In retrospect, the expressive role was reduced to function as only a breeding role. The man was not able to provide for his family, protect his family and/or socialize his children in any capacity. Lynch (1712):

"Understanding is the best thing, Therefore, we shall go deeper into this area of the subject matter concerning what we have produced here in this breaking process of the female nigger. We have reversed the relationships. In her natural uncivilized state she would have a strong dependency on the uncivilized nigger male, and she would have a limited protective tendency toward her independent male offspring and would raise the female offspring to be dependent like her. Nature had provided for this type of balance. We reversed nature by burning and pulling the civilized nigger apart and bull whipping the other to the point of death — all in her presence. By her being left alone, unprotected, with the male image destroyed, the ordeal caused her to move from her psychological dependent state to a frozen independent state. In this frozen psychological state of independence she will raise her male and female offspring in reversed roles. For fear of the young male's life, she will psychologically train him to be mentally weak and dependent but physically strong.

Because she has become psychologically independent, she will train her female offspring psychologically independent. What have we got? You've got the nigger woman out front and the man behind and scared. This is a perfect situation for sound sleep and economics."

The repositioning of roles made the black man the weaker role in the relationship due to his inability to protect and provide for his family. In addition, the cruelty administered in front of the women and children as well as the reversal of roles allowed the slave master to have more control over his slaves.

Morrow (2003) further expounds:

> *"We have, through four decades of conditioning been made to believe and practice a foreign peoples dictated life style. This Euro-centric practice of individual independence of man and woman makes it look like blacks are directly the sole cause of the destruction of their own family structure"* (p.30).

For the purpose of this book I am going to provide an historical perspective by taking a look at the slave period and the practices implemented to make slaves. These practices disrupted the attachment and trust in the intimate relationship between the African American man and woman as well as disrupted the socialization of children and stabilization of adult personality. I will evaluate and deconstruct the content in the Willie Lynch letter, for the reason that, whether the Lynch letter is true or not the letter substantiates practices carried out during the time of slavery. These practices continue to have adverse effects on the intimate relationship between African American men and women.

Psychohistory and Attachment Theory

*Can a people... live and develop over three hundred years
simply by reacting? Are American Negros simply the creation
of white men, or have they at least helped to create themselves
out of what they found around them?*

Ralph Ellison (1964)

Bowlby contends that attachment style has transgenerational transmission.
This is due to the parenting one experienced in childhood is passed down
to the next generation. If the parent had a secure attachment, it is expected
that their child would develop a secure attachment, through the parenting
behavior and patterns that is replicated to the child. Kurth (2013) wrote an
article discussing the psychohistorical aspects of attachment. Kurth wanted
to highlight the connection between the psychological and the sociological.
He believed that history and the culture of that time influenced a parent's
parenting behavior and interaction with their child. Marris (1991) states:

*"... our childhood experience of attachment... will
be influenced in turn by the child-rearing practices of a
culture. This is the first crucial link between sociological and
psychological understanding: the experience of attachment,
which so profoundly influences the growth of personality, is
itself both the product of a culture, and a determinant of how
a culture will be reproduced in the next generation—not only
the culture of attachment itself, but all our ideas or order,
authority, security, and control."* (p. 79).

What is being highlighted in the above passage is the influence the
macro-system has on the parenting behavior (micro-system) that will
ultimately influence the way a child's personality will develop. The family

does not rear a child in a bubble; whatever is happening in the world around them has an influence on the interaction between the parent and child. For example, during slavery parents were reluctant to show affection toward their children for fear of being separated from them; being beaten in front of them or killed. During that time in history, the culture did not permit the natural nurturing a parent may have given to their child when they were back home in Africa. Thus, psychohistory gives another explanation for the evolutionary roots of the theory. Parenting behavior has to be able to evolve and adjust to what is going on in history and the culture in order for the next generation to survive and be successful in connecting with others and understanding their environment. Therefore, where genes were identified as a way that biological structure is transmitted, the interaction between parent and child is the psychological structure that is transmitted. Kurth (2013) discusses *"collective-traumatizing"* historical events like World War II and the Post-Truamatic Stress Disorder (PTSD) veterans experienced and the different interactions they had with their family when they returned home. "The victims of camp imprisonment, torture, rape and bomb attacks imposed similar posttraumatic disturbances upon their families… In all these cases it becomes clear that the traumatic experience—also the experiences passed on to family members—affects not only the infant but can have attachment-relevant effects on every age level" (p. 107). In modern times children are rarely separated from their parents and harsh wars are not as prevalent. Parents today are physically present but emotionally unavailable due to work, school and/or running a business, thus being less available or unavailable for the children. Due to their unavailability parents showed limited sensitivity to their child's needs (Kurth, 2013). Research showed that marginalized families continue to experience long periods of separation and extreme lack of resources (Kurth, 2013).

The doctrine of slavery, applied by whites onto Africans, was a macro-system that had great influence on the parenting behavior of slaves. Those beliefs and teachings had a profound influence on the child's personality developed during that time.

Attachment theory will be used to explain what is needed to develop a secure attachment. By understanding what is needed we will then understand the attachment behavior that was disrupted to create an insecure attachment. The theory will identify the attachment style that will be inherited by the adult due to their childhood experience. This Attachment theory explains how the attachment style developed in childhood has a life-long impact on their future adult relationships.

Slave Practices

Cruel and brutal slave practices influenced parenting behavior. The punishment of slaves was carried out in front of the other slaves (women, men and children). The main function of slavery was to have power and to control over slaves. Frederick Douglass gives an account of a slave named Demby who was brutally punished in front of other slaves to set an example of what would happen to them if they were to behave like him:

> *"He was asked by Colonel Lloyd and my old master, why he resorted to this extraordinary expedient. His reply was, (as well as I can remember,) that Demby had become unmanageable. He was setting a dangerous example to the other slaves, -- one which, if suffered to pass without some such demonstration on his part, would finally lead to the total subversion of all rule and order upon the plantation. He argued that if one slave refused to be corrected, and escaped with his life, the other slaves would soon copy the example; the result of which would be the freedom of the slaves, and the enslavement of the whites"* (Andrews, Gates 2002, p. 296).

Descriptions provided by slaves of these practices, provide a vivid picture of what would happen if certain conduct and rules were not maintained by the slaves. Slaves could be beaten in front of other slaves at any time, for any unwanted behavior, interaction or rule violation.

Attachment Theory

Attachment theory was developed by John Bowlby, a British psychiatrist and psychoanalyst, who used a psychological model to explain the long-term emotional bond between a child and a parent, characterized by the tendency to seek and maintain closeness, especially during times of stress (Bowlby, 1969). Bowlby applied Ethology to study the natural attachment behavior of infants and their parents, primarily the mother, under near natural conditions; and viewing behavior as an evolutionary adaptive attribute. The theory evolved from not only explaining the behavior patterns of infants and children, but to include adolescents and adults (Bowlby, 1988). The theory will be used to provide an understanding of what characteristics of parent interaction with their child help to develop a healthy emotional bond; why this relationship is important for survival and its transgenerational effects. Bowlby believed, by understanding what develops a healthy emotional bond one could conclude that the absence or lack of it is what creates pathology in children. The pathology developed in childhood continues into adulthood and impacts how one engages in relationships with others and their expectations of others and the world. In addition, Bowlby understood the parent's childhood experience could influence their parenting behavior, thus determine the emotional bond that would develop between the parent and child. This emotional bond is most likely adopted by the child and is how they engage relationships and the world throughout the life-span.

The theory suggests that when a child is born, they have psychological needs that must be met, specifically food and warmth.

Through the mother providing food and warmth, which is meeting the psychological need, the child becomes attached to a human being, the mother. Bowlby (1969) states:

> *"There is in infants an in-built propensity to be in touch with and to cling to a human being. In this sense there is a 'need' for an object [**independent**] of food which is as primary as the 'need' for food and warmth... love has its origin in attachment"* (p. 178-179).

In the passage above, Bowlby highlights the innate propensity for infants to be close to and interact with a human being. This interaction is free of food and warmth, yet is necessary for building attachment. From birth to 6 weeks an infant's innate signal attract the mother to the infant. The mother remains close by when the infant responds positively. From 6 weeks to 6-8 months the infant develops a sense of trust that the mother will respond when signaled.

In this section, a summarization of attachment theory will be given; why attachment is important in healthy personality development; its survival component and its transgenerational effects.

Attachment Behavior

> *"Attachment behavior is regarded as a class of social behavior of an importance equivalent to that of mating behavior and parental behavior. It is held to have a biological function specific to itself and one that has hitherto been little considered"* (Bowlby, 1969, p. 179).

According to Bowlby attachment behavior is activated by the mother's departure or by anything that might frighten an infant such as: sound, sight or the mother's touch. During these situations proximity to the mother becomes important for protection and comfort. This behavior does not change during adolescence and adulthood; what changes are the figure to whom the behavior is directed. Attachment behavior is demarcated as the seeking and maintaining of proximity to another person.

Proximity

Proximity is an attachment behavior between a mother and child that is activated when an infant is frightened. When frightened the infant seeks his mother for physical closeness to reduce his fear. Proximity is kept by both the mother and the child. This behavior is developed through the interaction with their environment. The mother is the agent that provides the blueprint of the environment for her infant through their interaction. Restoring and maintain proximity is the attachment behavior used in the environment. Bowlby (1969) states "In species where the father plays a major role in upbringing it may come to be directed towards him as well. In humans it may be directed also towards a few others" (p.182). The attachment behavior in adolescence and adulthood is a parallel continuation from childhood. As a result, as long as close proximity is restored and maintained a child feels secure.

Nature and function of attachment behavior

Bowlby believed that the nature and function of attachment behavior was for evolutionary survival purpose. Attachment behavior protects children from harm. Through the interaction between parent and child, the child learns from the parent various activities necessary for survival. In the presence of the mother, a child is able to learn its environment, activities and other things valuable for the child's survival. The child learns by mimicking the parent; in addition, the parent directs the behavior to same items such as food. The direction from the mother provides learning for the child to determine what the food is in their environment. Proximity (attachment behavior) keeps the child close from harm and provides an opportunity for the child to learn valuable information, regarding survival, from the parent.

According to Bowlby (1973) attachment behavior has a homeostatic component. When the mother (attachment figure) is in close proximity stress levels, in the child is low. When the mother moves out of proximity the child's stress levels increase, thus activating attachment behavior, the child and mother begin to seek closeness to be in proximity of one another (p.149).

"This is because, so long as an individual remains within his familiar physical environment and with familiar companions, he is more likely than he would be otherwise to find food and drink, and to achieve reliable and continuing protection from natural hazards – from predators, from eating poisonous food-stuff, from falling and drowning, from exposure and cold. Conversely, so long as the systems maintaining physiology homeostasis are successful, the healthier will the individual be and the easier will it be for him to maintain himself effectively within his familiar environment" (Bowlby, 1973, p. 150).

Remaining within the familiar physical environment and amongst the child's parents helps keep the child's stress levels low and maintains psychological balance. In this respect, a child's attachment behavior serves as psychological and physical protection (Bowlby, 1969; Bowlby 1973).

Separation of Mother

A child's separation from his mother provokes fear and activates attachment behavior. Bowlby suggests there are three phases a child goes through when he is separated from his mother. Those phases are Protest, Despair and Detachment. Each phase has been observed to fuse into the next. The transition time that occurs between each phase could last days or weeks.

The first phase is Protest. During this phase the child appears to be in agony over the separation from his mother. The agony may be displayed immediately by the child or may be a delayed reaction. The child during this phase, may seek to find his mother through many different avenues (i. e. asking questions, looking out the window, searching the room). In addition, reactions the child may have are to cry loudly, throw himself around, look to any sight or sound that could possibly be his mother. All the behaviors are done in the expectation that his mother will return.

Despair is the second phase. In this phase, one can visibly see that the child still desires his missing mother through his continued behaviors. The child continues to be emotionally bothered by his mother's absence. The active searching for mother decreases or ceases to exist but he may still cry on occasion. The child may become withdrawn and inactive; there may be no demands made on people or the environment.

Last, is the Detachment phase, during this phase the child no longer rejects other people. The child will accept care from another person as well as food. If the mother is absent for a long period of time the child may not recognize her when she returns. When the mother reappears during this phase the normal attachment behavior is not present. When the child's mother enters the room the child may not know her; he may remain distant and indifferent towards her and there may not be tears for her but a turning away from her, as though he has lost all interest of her.

If a child continues to have the experience of becoming momentarily attached to different people due to them leaving and repeating the experience of his original loss of his mother; the child will eventually behave as if being mothered or having contact with humans is not a necessity in his life. After the experience of repeat losses of mother-figures to whom he has given trust and love, he will begin to seek these types of figures less and less, In addition, he will stop attaching himself to others. The presence or absence of a child's mother (parent) is what matters most in regards to attachment.

These experiences with the parent develops internal working models that the infant refers to when interacting with others. Berman & Sperling (1994) describe internal working models as:

> *"An internal working model is a representation in the mind that includes aspects of self, the attachment figure, situational invariants for attachment interactions, and the affects that connect the two figures. Internal working models are based on a prior history of attachment relationships plus current interactions between the self and the attachment figure when the attachment behavioral system is activated. In addition, internal working models define the rules by which two individuals interact, including behaviors, feelings, and thoughts. These rules allow each individual to anticipate and plan (correctly or incorrectly) what the other person will do a preceding set of actions... " (p.8).*

Internal working models are developed within the child through the experience he or she has with their parent(s). Those working models are with the child throughout adolescents and adulthood. The internal working models are the frame of reference that informs the child how others should be treated and how he will be treated by others. The experience with parents develops internal working models that influence the development of a secure or insecure attachment. In addition, through the lens of the internal working models, the child also has an expectation that others will treat him the way he or she was treated, by his parents, in childhood.

Fear of Separation

Fear of separation is described as inaccessibility of the parent either temporarily or permanently. Bowlby (1973) contends that:

> *"In view of this, it could be argued, an infant comes to learn that presence of mother is associated with comfort while absence of mother is associated with distress. Thus, through a fairly simple process of associative learning, an infant comes to associate mother's absence with distress, and so to fear her being inaccessible"* (p. 180).

Inaccessibility to the mother puts the child in distress due to fear that protection and care will not be provided which is a basic need for survival. The child has learned through interaction with the mother that she will provide and protect her young. The child becomes fearful of how will these basic needs be provided in her absence.

The child does not feel secure. Bowlby provides a distinction between feeling *secure* and feeling *safe*, in his writings. Feeling *secure* is how one feels in the world. Feeling secure in the world means one believes he will be cared for and he will be free of anxiety. *Safety* means being free from hurt or damage. "As such it applies to the world as it is and not the world as reflected in feeling" (Bowlby, 1973, p. 182).

A person who is acting as an attachment figure for another person, he or she is regularly referred to as providing the person with a sense of security. They become a secure base for the child because they are regularly accessible as well as in times of distress. According to this theory these attachment figures are described as "a security figure or as providing a secure base" (Bowlby, 1973, p.183).

Secure Attachment

Secure attachment is achieved through good enough mothering (parenting); it plays a major role in healthy personality development in children. When a parent is accessible and responsive to their child's needs, the child develops confidence that their needs will be met in the world.

What we have learned from the previous information is that the lack of an accessible and responsive parent creates an environment where the child grows up to be anxious and fearful, thus having an anxious attachment. Bowlby (1973) asserts:

> *"Similarly, the family experience of those who grow up to become relatively stable and self-reliant is characterized not only by unfailing parental support when called upon but also by a steady yet timely encouragement towards increasing autonomy"* (p. 322-323).

Mother's that are more attentive to their infant's signals and communication tend to respond more correctly. This produces a positive experience between the mother and child. The child learns that the mother will meet their needs when signaled.

The child is assured through this interaction that the mother will comfort him and ensure that the connection is kept.

The research conducted by Bowlby also showed that the patterns of parenting behavior towards children had transgenerational effects. The parenting experiences during childhood were repeated from generation to generation. The parenting behavior patterns learned, during childhood, is implemented when those children become adults.

> *"Because in all these respects children tend to unwittingly to identify with parents and therefore to adopt, when they become parents, the same patterns of behavior towards children that they themselves have experienced during their own childhood, patterns of interaction are transmitted, more or less faithfully, from one generation to the next"* (p.323).

Secure attachment is not only transmitted in parenting style but is also carried throughout the life-cycle in relationships with others. The attachment style, either anxious or secure is developed during childhood and is the way in which the person interacts with others and the world. A child that is securely attached has had a parent who has been accessible and responsive. Due to that experience, that child will provide the same parenting behavior pattern to their child thus developing a secure attached child. This style will be transmitted from generation to generation thus, according to this theory, creating in each generation secure attachment in each generation. Securely attached individuals believe that others as well as the world will meet their needs.

The components in the family that help to develop a secure attachment is the child living with both parents; the marriage being described as good and the child's childhood being described as being happy (Bowlby, 1973). The latter information helps the child learn who the accessible and responsive people are in their life as well as the environment in which those people are found. The study suggests that a secure family base is the foundation from which children, adolescents and young adults develop a secure attachment. Confidence is built in children when children receive a lot of support in their home; communication is clear between the parent and child and children and adolescents are given a lot responsibility. When a child or adolescent has a confident relationship with his family, the home is secure, supportive and encouraging, the child or adolescent is able to recreate that attachment with others and the world. When these components have been established and are active in the parent-child relationship, the child is more trustful of others and feels more confident to move confidently in their environment. This is because the child believes that the experience in childhood will be matched by the people he meets and comes into contact with in the world. Bowlby (1973) states:

"For not only young children, it is now clear, but human beings of all ages are found to be at their happiest and to be able to deploy their talents to best advantage when they are confident that, standing behind them, there are one or more trusted persons who will come to their aid should difficulties arise. The person trusted provides a secure base from which his (or her) **[companion]** *can operate"* (p.359).

It is clear that when a child develops a secure attachment, he or she, in adulthood is able to provide that to their companion thus being someone who is accessible and responsive to the other person. They are a person that is able to meet the needs of the other person and comfort that person in times of distress. Thus, the childhood experience is passed down in their adult relationships. A parent's own attachment experience influence the attachment style they pass on to their children. As adults, the needs we have as children do not disappear, we continue to depend on others and seek a trustful person that can help in troubled times. We seek someone or others to attach to, to continue the experience of feeling securely attached.

Attachment Figure

An attachment figure is a person that a child seeks proximity with when upset or threatened. The attachment figure is someone that the child has a deep emotional bond that connects the child to the attachment figure. The attachment figure is attentive to the child and responds sensitively and appropriately to the child's needs and fears. The child usually directs his behavior to his mother figure.

According to Bowlby (1973) "Whether a child or adult is in a state of security, anxiety, or distress is determined in large part by the accessibility and responsiveness of his principal attachment figure (p. 23)." The attachment figure helps in developing and maintaining the child's emotional state. If the primary childhood experiences is that of security that is the attachment style the child will have in adulthood; the same can be said with a childhood experience of a lot of anxiety. The child will have an anxious attachment style in adulthood. The attachment figure is vital to the emotional well-being and personality development of a child. The attachment figure helps the child learn about how their world will be and what the child can expect from others and the world.

Anxious (Insecure) attachment

Anxious attachment (also termed insecure attachment) is described as a parent who tends to be emotionally unavailable and unresponsive to their child's needs. The parent can be rejecting and/or disregard the child when they are hurt or sick. Anxious attachment develops through the experience the child has with his attachment figure. The child has no confidence that his attachment figure will be accessible and responsive when needing comfort; feeling fear and or threatened. Children with an anxious attachment live in a highly unpredictable world. Through interaction with their attachment figure the child has learned that this person is inaccessible and unresponsive to their needs. The child has also learned that the attachment figure's presence is very random, not predictable in any sense. According to Bowlby (1973) most young children become stressed when separated from their mother; this is most evident when the child is age 2 and 3 years of age (p. 222). Unstable homes where parents are either breaking up or not together contribute to an anxious attachment. Research showed that children who experienced unstable and inconsistent daily care from a caregiver, before the second birthday, showed signs of being insecure and anxious in later years (Bowlby, 1973).

Detachment

Detachment describes the way a child reacts to their attachment figure after being separated from her for a time period and then meets her again. Children who had been separated from their attachment figure for days or weeks, when reunited with their attachment figure showed detachment behaviors. Detachment behaviors are: no recognition of the attachment figure; turning away and/or walking away from the attachment figure; crying or coming close to crying; and an expressionless face. Furthermore, "There is reason to believe that after a very prolonged or repeated separation during the first three years of life detachment can persist indefinitely" (p.

12). From the above information we learn that separation is dangerous; it has lifelong effects and should be avoided if possible.

Secure Base

Parents are the secure base for their children; as a secure base the child is able to explore the world and is assured that when he returns the parent will be accepting and ready to care for the child emotionally and physically. In addition the parent provides comfort in times of fear and distress. As stated by Bowlby (1988):

> *"This brings me to a central feature of my concept of parenting—the provision by both parents of a secure base from which a child or adolescent can make sorties into the outside world and to which he can return knowing for sure that he will be welcomed when he gets there, nourished physically and emotionally, comforted if distressed, reassured if frightened"* (p.12).

A secure base is an attachment figure that has a relationship with the child who meets the child's needs and who the child can turn to for safety. The secure base helps the child to manage their anxiety. When the secure base is accessible and responsive the child's anxiety is reduced and they can enjoy and explore the world. They explore the world with confidence that he can return to the secure base for help if needed. Adults as well as children need a secure base as they move through the life span. Adults form new attachments with friends and romantic partners; these relationships serve the same function for adults as they did for the children. Family, friends and romantic partners serve as a secure base for adults. Their function is to be accessible and responsive to the person's needs. To provide comfort, emotional and physical support.

When family, friends and/or romantic partners are accessible they help the adult to reduce stress. These people provide the adult confidence to maneuver throughout the world.

> *"All of us, from the cradle to the grave, are happiest*
> *when life is organized as a series of excursions, long or short,*
> *from the secure base provided by our attachment figures"*
> (Bowlby, 1988).

Bowlby believed that the children and adolescents that were the most emotionally stable and made the most of their opportunities was due to them having accessible, responsible comforting parents.

Caring for Children

Many people have a strong desire to have children and to help them develop into happy, healthy, well-mannered, emotionally healthy children. There is a lot of pressure and expectation about raising children and being an active parent in the child's life. Bowlby (1988) states "Furthermore, because, successful parenting is a principal key to the mental health of the next generation. The ways in which we care for children is important for the child's personality development and emotional health. The experience a child has in childhood will be passed down to the next generation…"(p.1). There is a high expectation about the ways in which parents care for their children to develop children that are emotionally and physically healthy. Caring for children is an innate fundamental practice that has historical roots and is expected for the following generations.

Being a parent is a great deal of tough work that requires lots of patience and creativity. As children grow older their needs do not decrease they merely shift. Being a parent means that one has to sacrifice some of their interests for their children to parent appropriately. Children require a good deal of attention and care to become confident, independent adults who are able to develop healthy relationships with others. When parents are actively involved with caring for their children they may have to decline or put off certain activities until their children are more independent. Bowlby believed that parenting was a lot for one person and that to do it properly the person would need lots of assistance from others but primarily the other parent. Children require a great deal of time and attention and one person may not have enough resources within them and/or enough patience to provide a child with the parenting he needs. Utilizing others as a resource is helpful when caring for children. Caring for children is what develops the type of attachment bond a child will have with his parent(s). When a child is feeling frightened, tired and or pain attachment behavior is activated. The child seeks the mother for comfort. The mother's biological function is that of protection. As children grow into adolescents and then adults this behavior does not cease... the behavior may be directed to other attachment figures. The accessibility and appropriate response from the parent, to the child, develops a sense of security for the child. The foundation of a person's parenting comes from their own childhood experience. Through the childhood experience a child learns that caring for children involves the following activities: reproduction, protection, nutrition and knowledge of the environment.

Bowlby (1988) observed the interaction between mother and child after child birth. He recognized that mother's naturally pick up the child after child birth and strokes his face with her fingertips. She then proceeds to touch his head and body, in addition, she is likely to put the infant to her breast. As soon as a baby is born the mothers attention becomes fixed on the baby (p.7). The next few days with the baby is spent looking at the baby; cuddling with the baby and getting to know his temperament. Through the activity of parenting children can be either attached or not attached to both parents dependent on how they treat their child. When a child has a secure relationship with their mother and father, the child, is more confident and competent than children who do not have this type of relationship (Bowlby, 1988). According to the theory a mother needs to be in harmony with her child's actions and signals and responds to them appropriately.

In addition, the mother needs to be able to monitor how her response impacts the child and to modify and adjust accordingly. Bowlby believed a relaxed atmosphere, that provided enough time, is the best environment to nurture this type of preferred parenting to create a securely attached child.

Influence of parents childhood experience

Research showed that the feelings mother's had toward their children was a direct reflection of their personal childhood experience. This evidence supports the transgenerational impact attachment has on the next generation. The parenting behaviors one received in their childhood is what will be provided to their child and passed down as a way of caring for children. How the parent responds to the child in times of distress is what the child learns and in future situations will respond the same way. An example is when a child hurts himself, how the parent responds is how the child will most likely respond in similar situations in the future. If the parent is frantic and overly concerned the child will have the same reaction. In general, what a child does in certain situations is a direct reflection of what he has observed or experienced his mother or primary caregiver doing (Bowlby, 1988).

Successful parenting requires that the parent gives a great deal of their time and attention, so that the child develops a secure attachment and is able to mimic and/or expect the experiences in childhood with others over the life span. The tools for successful parenting are:

> *"… we seek always to teach by example, not precept, by discussion, not instruction. The more that we can give young people opportunities to meet with and observe at firsthand how sensitive, caring parents treat their offspring. The more likely they are to follow suit"* (Bowlby, 1988, p. 17-18).

How we parent and treat our children is extremely essential to what a child believes he can expect from others and the world. Parenting teaches the child about his environment; the child learns what areas are safe in his environment and what areas are unsafe. Children gain confidence that they will be cared for through experiences they have with their parents. The child learns that in times of distress this person can restore balance and help in reducing anxiety by being a secure base from which he can explore the world. Parenting is a fundamental experience that sets the child up to have either a secure or anxious attachment to others. Furthermore, their childhood experience is what will be replicated with their children.

Role of Attachment on Personality Development

Next, we will discuss the role of attachment on personality development. One of the expectations in parenting children is that they are emotionally healthy. Bowlby has identified that good-enough mothering is the avenue to meet that expectation. Not only does the parent want to accomplish this for their child while they are young but they want their child to be emotionally healthy as adolescents and adulthood. Through the interaction of the parent the child learns how others are supposed to treat him and how he is to treat others.

Humans have an innate desire to have an emotional connection to others. This desire humans have to connect has been observed while the child is still in his mother's womb all the way through adulthood. When a child is first born and through childhood the bonds are with the parents (or parent substitutes). These persons are sought for protection, comfort and support. In adolescents and adulthood, these bonds continue, but are directed less toward parents and more towards others. Bowlby states that in the beginning the bond between the mother and child are maintained through "emotionally mediated communication" (Bowlby, 1988, p. 136). This type of communication and intimate relationship continues throughout life. A person's ability to want to seek out others and act in either the care-seeking role or the care-giving role is an example of effective personality functioning and mental health. The child learned these behaviors from the parenting they received in childhood, which afforded them to be able to offer these attributes to others. The capacity for one to either be a caregiver or to be care-seeking is a direct reflection of attachment behavior experienced during childhood. How close one is willing to get to another person is also a direct reflection of the attachment behavior and bond in the childhood experience. Bowlby (1988) states that when a person feels secure he is more willing to explore his environment and the opportunities it has to offer (p.137). An example is young adults who have a secure attachment with their family are more likely to leave home and explore education, work and intimate relationships with others.

Those with a more anxious attachment are more reluctant to explore because through their childhood experience they have learned that he or she may not receive protection, comfort and support.

> *"The presence of an attachment control system and its linkage to the working models of self and attachment figure (s) that are built in the mind during childhood are held to be central features of personality functioning throughout life"* *(Bowlby, 1988, p. 139).*

The way a child is treated by his parents during childhood (infancy and childhood) deeply influences the attachment pattern he or she will have over their life span. There are three types of attachment: secure attachment; anxious resistant attachment and anxious avoidant attachment. Bowlby describes these attachment styles as:

> *"These are first the pattern of secure attachment in which the individual is confident that his parent (or parent figure) will be available, responsive, and helpful should he encounter adverse or frightening situations. With this assurance, he feels bold in his explorations of the world. This pattern is promoted by a parent, in the early years especially by mother being readily available, sensitive to her child's signals, and lovingly responsive when he seeks protection and/or comfort.*
>
> *A second pattern is that of anxious resistant attachment in which the individual is uncertain whether his parent will be available or responsive or helpful when called upon. Because of this uncertainty he is always prone to separation anxiety, tends to be clinging, and is anxious about exploring the world. This pattern, in which conflict is evident, is promoted by a parent being available and helpful on some occasions but not on others, and by separations and as clinical findings show, by threats of abandonment used as a means of control.*

> *A third pattern is that of anxious avoidant attachment in which the individual has no confidence that, when he seeks care, he will be responded to helpfully, but, on the contrary, expects to be rebuffed. When in marked degree such an individual attempts to live his life without the love and support from others, he tries to become emotionally self-sufficient... This pattern, in which conflict is more hidden, is the result of the individual's mother constantly rebuffing him when he approaches her for comfort or protection. The most extreme cases result from repeated rejection"* (Bowlby, 1988, p. 140).

Personality development, in the child, is greatly impacted by the mother child interaction. The mother's ability to be responsive or non-responsive is what develops the attachment style. If the interaction was consistent and reliable the child develops a secure attachment. If the interaction was inconsistent, he will develop an anxious resistant attachment. Lastly, if the child experiences rejection from the mother and his needs are not met, the child will develop an anxious avoidant attachment.

During slavery, children experienced an absent mother who was prohibited from caring, comforting and protecting her children. The attachment developed during this time may have been an anxious avoidant attachment. This attachment style would be passed from generation to generation.

Attachment During the Period of Slavery

In this section, attachment theory will be used to provide an understanding of the attachment rupture that occurred during the implementation process of slavery in the United States and its transgenerational effects, as well as an explanation for why African American romantic couples have trouble staying together due to the historical attachment rupture that occurred. A focus will be placed on the following areas: attachment behavior; caring for children and attachment styles, to understand the attachment bond that was inherited from the generations of African Americans following slavery.

According to the theory, the components in the family that help to develop a secure attachment is the child living with both parents; the marriage being described as good and the child's childhood being described as being happy (Bowlby, 1973). During slavery, marriage was constructed by the slave owner for the purpose of creating good economics not to produce healthy whole families. Marriage was approached in the form of breeding not for the purpose of emotional bonding and developing happy, healthy, well-mannered securely attached children. Marriage between slaves replicated the breeding of animals. Slave owners married two slaves they believed would produce more strong saleable slaves. In this section the marriage during slavery will be discussed and the ways in which the disruption of the family prevented parents and children from engaging in attachment behavior and emotional bonding.

Before we discuss the attachment behavior and emotional bonding between parent and child… we must first take a look back at what was happening during the time of slavery and decisions that were being made due to the issue of the declining slave population. Plantation owners noticed that the Africans were dying due to not being used to the new environment, which was causing a decrease in the slave population. In addition, the cost of importing slaves from Africa was becoming increasingly more and more expensive. Lastly, conversations, amongst leaders, were being held to abolish the trans-Atlantic Slave Trade. The discussion of breeding American slaves had become a primary topic of discussion to decrease cost and replenish and produce slaves. The decision to breed slaves would be another contributing factor for the attachment rupture that occurred in this group of people. During this period of time, the purpose of breeding was not to build strong family connections between mother and child; the purpose was for maintaining and increasing production. In addition, the goal in breeding these people was to produce slaves that were strong, healthy laborers.

It is probable that the Willie Lynch speech may have been given in 1712 this would have been 77 years before the Committee of the Privy Council began discussions regarding the abolition of the Atlantic Slave Trade in 1789. What we know to be true is, North Americans noticed a decline in their slave population and in addition, noticed the costly expense of importing slaves and needed a solution. The Willie Lynch letter indicates a blueprint for breeding slaves to not only produce slaves but to increase the growth of slaves and to condition the mind of the slave to be obedient to the master. The letter suggests that if these practices were implemented they would perpetuate for 300 years. The Willie Lynch letter appears to demonstrate a creation of a blueprint that other plantation owners could use to ensure they would maintain and grow strong healthy laborers.

American slave owners considered women as *"propagation"* machines; this means women were considered as animals used to reproduce more animals like themselves for monetary reasons (Donoghue, 2008). At this time in history in America, there was a dramatic decrease in the cultivation of land for tobacco and an increasing demand for the production of cotton.

"North American cotton production increased from 3,000 bales in 1790 to 178,000 bales in 1810. Production skyrocketed to 732,000 bales in 1830 and to 4.5 million bales in 1860. To take advantage of the economic boom, planters rushed to settle in Georgia, Alabama, Mississippi, Louisiana and Texas, that contained soil ideal for cotton cultivation." (Fogel & Engerman, 1974, p. 44).

Marriage during Slavery

During the slavery period there were several ways the slave master constructed marriages and families to perpetuate the disruption of the family and the ability of the men, women and children to attach and bond. Practices implemented such as the Niggar Marriage (plantation marriage); Sale and Relocation of families; Abroad Marriages and Biological Alienation. Marriage on the plantation was manufactured, it was not a civil union where to individuals and/or families decided that this man and woman should be married. To control the attachment and bond to one another the slave master determined who married; their living arrangement and their sexual interactions.

Plantation Marriage

Plantation marriages also known as Niggar Marriages were determined by the slave master. The sole purpose for allowing two slaves to marry was to ensure the creation of the same type of strong slave. Slave masters wanted strong male and female slaves to ensure good economics. Lynch (1712) describes the practice of the niggar marriage as follows:

> *"We breed two nigger males with two nigger females. Then we take the nigger males away from them and keep them moving and working. Say one nigger female bears a nigger female and the other bears a nigger male. Both nigger females being without influence of the nigger male image, frozen with an independent psychology, will raise their offspring into reverse positions. The one with the female offspring will teach her to be like herself, independent and negotiable (we negotiate with her, through her, by her, we negotiate her at will). The one with the nigger male offspring, she being frozen with a subconscious fear for his life, will raise him to be mentally dependent and weak, but physically strong, in other words, body over mind. Now in a few years when these two offspring's become fertile for early reproduction we will*

mate and breed them and continue the cycle. That is good,
sound, and long range comprehensive planning."

In the passage above marriage is between two random male slaves and two random female slaves. Although labeled as "Niggar Marriage" what is being performed is breeding. During that time the Bible was used to brainwash the mind of the slave. According to the Bible when two people came together and had sex they were considered to be married. This practice was anything but... after sex many slaves never saw each other again due to working on different plantations. Next, the passage explains that once the two slaves have sexual intercourse the males are taken away kept moving and working to eliminate any attachment or bonding that could occur. Slaves were not allowed to have love relationships. They could be severely punished if the slave-owner found out two slaves where romantically interested in one another.

~Frederick Douglass~
"Aunt Hester went out one night, -- where or for what
I do not know, -- and happened to be absent when my
master desired her presence. He had ordered her not to go
out evenings, and warned her that she must never let him
catch her in the company with a young man, who was paying
attention to her, belonging to Colonel Lloyd... Aunt Hester
had not only disobeyed his orders in going out, but had been
found in company with Lloyd's Ned... Before he commenced
whipping Aunt Hester, he took her into the kitchen, and
stripped her from neck to waist, leaving her neck, shoulders,
and back, entirely naked. He then told her to cross her hands,
calling her at the same time a d---b b----h. After crossing
her hands, he tied them with a strong rope, and led her to a
stool under a large hook in the joist, put in for the purpose.
He made her get upon the stool, and tied her hands to the
hook. She now stood fair for his infernal purpose. Her arms
were stretched up at the full length, so that she stood upon the
ends of her toes. He then said to her, "Now, you d---b b---h,
I'll learn you how to disobey my orders!" and after rolling up
his sleeves, he commenced to lay on the heavy cowskin, and

> *soon the warm, red blood (amid heart rending shrieks from her, and horrid oaths from him) cam dripping to the floor"* (Andrews & Gates, 2002, p. 285).

The above is one account of many that slaves experienced frequently throughout slavery. Harriet Ann Jacobs, a former slave, describes a time when she dared to love another slave. In the book *"Slave Narratives,"* in the section called *"The Lover"* Harriet recounts this experience. She informs the reader that she falls for a colored carpenter who is a free man. They had known each other since childhood. He loved her and she loved him… he wanted to marry Harriet. Her slave was a free man that wanted to buy her so that he could marry her. Harriet knew that her slave master and his wife would never allow that to happen. In addition, slave laws would not allow them to marry. Harriet states that she feared Mr. Flint's, her slave owner, punishment if he learned of her desires. If Harriet were to marry the free man he would have no power to protect her because the master's power superseded the husbands as long as she was not a free slave. Harriet explained that whites believed that slaves did not have a right to family ties that all their attention and affection should be for their owners. Harriet states that she found the courage to tell her master that she wanted to marry this free man. Following is a recount of this conversation:

> *"Do you love this nigger? He said abruptly…"Yes, sir."*
> *"How dare you tell me so!" He exclaimed, in great wrath…*
> *If I ever know of your speaking to him, I will cowhide you both; and if I catch him lurking about my premises, I will shoot him as soon as I would a dog. Do you hear what I say? I'll teach you a lesson about marriage and free niggers! Now go, and let this be the last time I have occasion to speak to you on this subject"* (Andrews & Gates, 2002, p. 785-786).

Later in the text we learn that Harriet told her lover to leave for Savannah, where his uncle had left him property, and to forget about her and never come back. Instances like these happened often where two slaves, who loved each other, could not express and engage in a relationship with one another. Thus, this is another example of cruel punishments used, threatened to obstruct marriage between slaves.

Mothers were not allowed to bond with their children. The mother would return to work and the child was placed in a plantation nursery. Provision in the plantation nursery was minimal and the care for the children was infrequent.

> *~Frederick Douglass~*
> *"The allowance of the slave children was given to their mothers, or the old women having the care of them. The children unable to work in the field had neither shoes, stockings, jackets, nor trousers, given to them; their clothing consisted of two coarse linen shirts per year. When these failed them they went naked until the next allowance-day. Children from seven to ten years old, of both sexes, almost naked, might be seen at all seasons of the year"* (Andrews & Gates, 2002, p. 287).

Under slavery in colonial America, parents were prohibited from caring for their own children, a role that was taken over by the slave owner. They were also taken away from their husband or wife and most times never seen them again.

> *~Olaudah Equiano – The African~*
> *"Why are parents to lose their children, brothers their sisters, or husbands their wives? Surely this is a new refinement in cruelty, which, while it has no advantage to atone for it, thus aggravates distress, and adds fresh horrors even to the wretchedness of slavery"* (Andrews & Gates, 2002, p.79).

Attachment Behavior

Attachment behavior is characterized as being activated by the mother's departure or by anything that might frighten the child. When the latter occurs proximity to the mother is very important for protection and comfort of the child. Attachment behavior was not allowed to be established during slavery. The slave owner did not want bonds to be created on the plantation for fear that if these bonds were developed, slaves would come together and revolt against the slave owner. Slaves were products to be sold and where needed for free labor and to build economics. Emotional and affectional bonds, put that practice at risk due to a natural propensity for a person to protect that which he or she has a deep emotional bond. Slave owners prevented bonds between males and females, husband and wife, parents and children through extremely long workdays; forced labor migrations; sales of slaves; use of plantation nurseries; abroad marriages and brutal punishment practices. Slave owners did not see any benefit in strengthening the bond between parents and their children. When women had their children they were forced to go back to work right after giving birth. They were not able to protect their children or to comfort them. Children were left with little or no adult supervision during the day while adults were working. One slave stated "During slavery, it seemed lak yo' chillum b'long to ev'ybody but you" (Dunaway, 2003, p. 1). Many times children were permanently separated from their mother and sold many times to different plantations. Conversely, approximately two-thirds of slave sales carried out separated children from their families and over 70 percent of these forced situations occurred before the child reached the age of fifteen (Dunaway, 2013). Children did not have an opportunity to bond and recognize their mother, therefore, attachment behavior may or may not have been activated but if activated, may not have been due to the mother's departure. In addition, fathers were rarely sold with their wife and children (Dunaway, 2003). If slave families were together, it was without the presence of the father. Mother and child bonding put the slave owners economics at risk and during that time slaves were more profitable than tobacco, grains and livestock due to the labor one received from owning slaves.

> *"Despite their own family ideals, Appalachian masters and mistresses constructed an ethnocentric ideology grounded in the assumptions that slaves did not construct permanent marriages, did not establish strong emotional ties to their children, or did not value extended kinship networks. In addition, the disadvantages to disrupted families were denied since the slave's "strongest affection" was purposed to be "love*

of his master, his guide, protector, friend," not ties to black kin" (Dunaway, 2013, p. 53).

In many situations slave sales involved many children being sold from their parents. Many children lived in a household alone without their parents (Dunaway, 2013). Attachment behavior is important for protection and comfort of the child by the mother. This behavior was blocked during slavery; there was no stable presence of a mother on a daily basis. Slave owners developed a childcare system that prevented mother and child from bonding. A child was placed in a plantation nursery with numerous other children and minimal supervision or care; this situation put these children at risk of injury, malnourishment and deficient psychological development (Dunaway, 2013).

Proximity

Proximity is an attachment behavior that is characterized by mother and child maintaining closeness so the child can be comforted when frightened. Proximity helps the child to reduce their fear by keeping physical closeness to his mother. The mother also provides the blueprint for their environment to teach the child what is safe and what is unsafe. During slavery mothers were prevented from keeping proximity to their children as a way to keep bonds from forming. Children from age 0-15 were often separated from their mothers through slave trades and slave sells. According to Dunaway (2013) "Nearly one of every three slave children living in the Upper South in 1820 was "sold South" by 1860" (p.20). Many households during slavery consisted of adult and children that were not related (Dunaway, 2013). Forced migrations were another way that children were separated from their mothers; a majority of children had this experience before the age of fifteen (Dunaway, 2013). When a child became frightened during slavery, he would not be able to engage in proximity behavior due to the mother not being on the same plantation or due to intentional separation by the slave owner. Attachment behavior may have been activated but proximity was not possible due to them being separated by either forced migration; being sold, traded or experienced brutal punishment practices.

Nature and function of attachment behavior

The nature and function of attachment behavior, according to Bowlby is about survival. Attachment behavior protects children from harm. The mother teaches the child about their environment.

The mother identifies enemies for the child; she teaches the child what areas are safe and unsafe and the mother teaches the child what food is and where to find it. The child learns to mimic the parent and the parent guides the child's behavior. This interaction helps the child to be safe and successful in the world. The child in turn will be able to teach their child the same information and provide the same protection. During slavery mothers were not able to protect their children. They were not able to guide their behavior. Mothers had to work 14 hour days a majority of their time was used for labor, which left little to no time for training her children (Dunaway, 2013). Slave owners replaced the mother's child-rearing. Slave owners placed infants and children in plantation nurseries. "Appalachian masters also intruded into motherhood through the formation of child care strategies that weakened the bonds between family members and placed young children at increased risk of malnutrition, injury, and inadequate psychological development" (Dunaway, 2013, p. 69). Mothers were not able to check on their children while they were in the nursery. Mothers were also not able to stay with their child if he or she was sick. Dunaway (2013) states:

> *"On the one hand, masters, not mothers, made fundamental decisions about the nature of child care: when, where, by whom, how much or how little? On the other hand, enslaved mothers did not have the option of not reporting to work when their children needed attention. Mothers risked punishment of children if they demanded better child care when the master's arrangement endangered their offspring. If the mother's caregiving conflicted with the master's work, she was required to do her "productive" work, most often in the fields or at nonagricultural sites" (p. 70).*

Slave owners receive minimal benefit from building bonds between parent and child. The goal of the master was to socialize the child to have an allegiance and obedience to the slave owner. Slave children were left with little or no adult supervision during the work days (Dunaway, 2013). By the time children were able to walk and take direction, usually long before age 10, they were assigned work by the slave owner.

> *"At age five, Sally Brown was taught to hoe, and she was expected to "keep rat up with the others, 'cause they'd tell [her] if [she] got behin that a run-a-way [slave] would get [her] and split open [her] head and git the milk out'a it"* (Dunaway, 2013, p. 72-73).

Proximity was forbidden to keep the bond between mother and child from forming. In addition, this interference, from the slave owner, did not allow the mother to provide the blueprint for the child's environment for survival purposes. When her child was frightened she was not able to keep proximity to aid in reducing his fear. The mother was prevented from guiding her child's behavior. During slavery proximity behavior was not permitted, thus putting the child at risk of harm and lack of protection; most of all no affectional bond.

Separation of Mother

Slavery was a time when children were routinely separated from their mothers. According to Bowlby, when a child is separated from his mother it activates attachment behavior. The three phases a child goes through when separated from their mother is *Protest, Despair* and *Detachment.* For the period of slavery, children were separated from their mothers without the ability to bond. Mothers were forced to work from sun up to sun down. Some slave owners only allowed the mother an hour a day to breastfeed half hour in the morning and half hour in the evening (Donoghue, 2008). The slave owner recognized the importance of the child receiving breast milk for mortality purposes. Infants were dying within the first twelve or fourteen days after birth (Donoghue, 2008). The child may have sought for someone and/or had an innate feeling that someone should be available when he was alone. Fear of separation from the mother may not have been a component or an experience understood due to separation occurring so early in infancy.

The second phase Despair may have existed. During this phase, one can visibly see that the child still desires his missing mother and is emotionally bothered. The child may not have these feelings for his mother but internally feels this need for someone to be available.

The last phase is Detachment. Detachment behavior is described as no recognition of the attachment figure; turning away and/or walking away from the attachment figure; crying or coming close to crying; and an expressionless face. Throughout this phase the child no longer rejects others but is receptive to comfort and protection from other people. For the duration of slavery children may have sought other children in the plantation nursery for comfort and protection. According to the theory detachment can be infinite if a child experiences long separations or repeated separations in the first three years of life (Bowlby, 1988). Slave children may have transitioned more quickly through phase one and two but were cemented indefinitely in the detachment phase. In line with the theory, children who experience repeat losses of mother-figures, whom he has given trust and love, he will begin to seek these types of figures less and less. He will stop attaching himself to others and determine that having contact with humans is not a necessity. This is the internal working model the child will refer to and inform his expectation of relationships throughout adolescents and adulthood.

~Frederick Douglass~
*"My mother and I were separated when I was but an infant – before I knew her as my mother. It is a common custom, in the part of Maryland from which I ran away, to part children from their mothers at a very early age. Frequently, before the child has reached its twelfth month, its Mother is taken from it, and hired out on some farm a considerable distance off, and the child is placed under the care of an old woman, too old for field labor. **[For what this separation has done, I don't know, unless it be to hinder the development of the child's affection toward its mother, and to blunt and destroy the natural affection of the mother for the child. This is the inevitable result]**" (Andrews & Gates, 2002, p. 281-282).*

Fear of Separation

Fear of separation is described as inaccessibility of the parent either temporarily or permanently. Bowlby (1973) contends that:

> *"In view of this, it could be argued, an infant comes to learn that presence of mother is associated with comfort while absence of mother is associated with distress. Thus, through a fairly simple process of associative learning, an infant comes to associate mother's absence with distress, and so to fear her being inaccessible"* (p. 180).

Inaccessibility to the mother puts the child in distress due to fear that protection and care will not be provided which is a basic need for survival. For the period of slavery, children of slaves did not have access to their mothers or fathers. These children lived in constant distress due to fear that protection and care would not be provided. Protection and care are a basic need for survival. The child has learned through his experience with the slave owner and life on the plantation that his mother, or any other person, is prohibited from providing or protecting their young. The child becomes fearful of how he will receive these basic needs and who will provide them in the mother's absence.

The child does not feel secure. As referenced earlier in the text, Bowlby provides a distinction between feeling *secure* and feeling *safe*, in his writings. Feeling *secure* is how one feels in the world. Feeling secure in the world means one believes he will be cared for and he will be free of anxiety. *Safety* means being free from hurt or damage. "As such it applies to the world as it is and not the world as reflected in feeling" (Bowlby, 1973, p. 182). From the brutal physical punishment slaves endured, we can contend that slave children did not feel safe in the world. Furthermore, Slave children did not feel secure in the world. These children did not believe they would be cared for, thus, were not free of anxiety. These children were not able to develop a secure attachment to their mother or anyone else for that matter. Based upon this theory, secure attachment is not only passed down through the parenting style but is carried throughout the life-cycle. For these children an anxious attachment style was developed during childhood. As these children grew into adults, this attachment style is the internal working model they used to interact with others and the world. Moreover, this attachment style was transmitted from generation to generation thus, according to this theory creating in each generation an anxious avoidant attachment in each family.

Fear of separation during slavery was a constant fear for mother and child. Slaves were like cattle, products to be sold and to be used for labor. Slave owners were not invested in building the bond between the mother and child. Children could be sold for more money than adults and children sold more quickly than adult slaves (Donoghue, 2008). By age five or six children were capable of labor and were sold to other plantation owners for labor (Donoghue, 2008). "American slaveholders considered slave women as propagation machines and encouraged reproduction for pecuniary reasons… No familial connections were mentioned in any significant detail and the concern was with the woman as a breeding machine" (Donoghue, 2008, p. 360). Slaves were sold every day; children were placed in plantation nurseries after birth and mothers were only able to see their child an hour a day; furthermore many infants died in the first twelve to fourteen days… fear of separation was a constant fear that was in existence during this time.

Attachment figure

An attachment figure is a person that a child seeks proximity with when upset or threatened. The attachment figure is someone that the child has a deep emotional bond that connects the child to the attachment figure. The attachment figure is attentive to the child and responds sensitively and appropriately to the child's needs and fears. A mother figure is usually the person the behavior is directed to. The attachment figure is vital to the emotional well-being and personality development of a child. The attachment figure helps the child learn about how their world will be and what the child can expect from others and the world.

Children born into slavery had no attachment figure. Their mother's primary purpose was to be breeding machines and provide labor for the slave owner (Donoghue, 2008). Their fathers were used as breeders and laborers, moved about from plantation to plantation. Henry Bibb a former slave states "It is almost impossible for slaves to give a correct account of their male parentage" (Andrews & Gates, 2002, p. 441). Children were placed in plantation nurseries, where the slave owner determined the type of care the children would receive. These nurseries were over populated with children and lacked adult supervision. Many times the nurseries had two adult slaves that were either very old or ill and unable to care for the children. The slave owner did not provide enough food and provision for the children which caused many children to experience malnutrition and injury. There was no one for the child to develop a deep emotional bond. Moreover there was no one as an attachment figure to be attentive to the child and respond sensitively and appropriately to the child's needs and fears. Dr. David Collins wrote a book about the medical management of slaves. In the book he suggests a practice to wean children from their mother sooner by instructing the overseers to implement that nurses keep a baby away from his mother day and night (Collins, 1971). In this passage we learn of another barrier put in place to block the natural bonding of mother and child through the use of nurses. A practice was implanted that put in place a random slave woman who was still producing milk to nurse the children in the plantation. The hour a day the mother used to get to nurse her child was no longer permitted. The practice that was implemented was intentional in cutting off the bond and interaction thus contributing to the attachment rupture between the mother and child. My great grandmother told me when I was little that other women nursed and watched over children during slavery... that during that time mother and child were not allowed to be together. This is a story that stuck with me for a long time. She also told me that many times white women did not want to nurse their own babies and many believed that slave milk was more nutritious than any other milk and therefore slaves were forced nurse white children as well. Plantation nurseries provided minimal supervision for children the persons that oversaw the nurseries were directed to keep the children away from their mothers. These children may have used each other as attachment figures but a consistent adult was not present for children when upset or threatened.

Anxious/insecure attachment

Anxious attachment (also termed insecure attachment) develops due to a parent's tendency to be emotionally unavailable and unresponsive to their child's needs. The parent can be rejecting and/or disregard the child when they are hurt or sick.

The child has no confidence that his attachment figure will be accessible and responsive when needing comfort; feeling fear and or threatened. Children with an anxious attachment live in a highly unpredictable world. Through interaction with their attachment figure the child has learned that this person is inaccessible and unresponsive to their needs. The child has also learned that the attachment figure's presence is very random, not predictable in any sense.

The attachment style developed throughout slavery was an anxious (insecure) attachment. Parents during slavery were made to work extremely long days; were sold and traded. According to Dunaway (2003) "… nearly two-thirds of all Appalachian slave sales separated children from their families…" (p.67). These children grew up with emotionally unavailable and unresponsive parents who were not allowed to tend to their child's needs nor comfort them when they felt fear; were hurt or sick. Many children lived with their white slave owner absent both parents (Dunaway, 2003). "… slave children were left with little to no adult supervision during the workdays" (Dunaway, 2003, p. 70). Attachment figures during this time were not available to the children. Adult slaves worked long arduous days. Their days began at 3am in the fields and their day in the field ended at 6:30pm, this was not a complete end to the work day as many slaves had to cut grass and care for the farm animals after working in the fields all day (Donoghue, 2008). Children were left in plantation nurseries, there was minimal supervision for the children; in addition the overseer of the nursery was usually a very old very sick adult slave.

Secure Base

According to this theory, parents are the secure base for their children. Parents, as the secure base, provide a stable foundation for the child to explore the world. The child has confidence that if he leaves his mother she will be there when he returns accepting and ready to care for him. The child has learned from interaction with the parent that as his secure base when he returns his parent will take care of him emotionally and physically.

A secure base is an attachment figure that has a relationship with the child who meets the child's needs and who the child can turn to for safety. The secure base helps the child to manage their anxiety. When the secure base is accessible and responsive the child's anxiety is reduced and they can enjoy and explore the world. They explore the world with confidence that he can return to the secure base for help if needed. Adults as well as children need a secure base as they move through the life span. Adults form new attachments with friends and romantic partners; these attachments serve the same function for adults as they did for the children. Family, friends and romantic partners serve as a secure base for adults. Their function is to be accessible and responsive to the person's needs. They provide comfort, emotional and physical support. When family, friends and/or romantic partners are accessible they help the adult to reduce stress.

For the period of slavery… women, men and especially children did not have a secure base to provide a stable foundation for them. The bond between a mother and child was weakened due to the mother being hired out or assigned to work for other plantations far away from her child. The long distance made it impossible for a mother to see her child, oftentimes mother and child never saw each other again (Dunaway, 2003). Slave owners believed it was futile to allow slaves to bond. They believed their sole purpose was to serve them; to be laborers to produce good economics. Moreover slave owners feared slaves bonding and coming together to kill them for the cruel practices, lies and separations during slavery.

Caring for Children

In Africa, raising children was an important part of developing the family and passing on tradition. "The family is at once the most sensitive, important, and enduring element in the culture of any people" (Billingsley, 1968, p. 38). Caring for children was shared between the mother and father. "The father played a very important role in the care and protection of the children in all these West African societies" (Billingsley, 1968, p.43). The expectation is for children to be strongly attached to their mother and that this attachment would carry over into adulthood. From their fathers they would learn morality; their civic duties and economic training. "Negros were forcibly uprooted from a long history of strong family and community life every bit as viable as that of their captors" (Billingsley, 1968, p. 38).

Africans took pride in caring for their children due to their children being a depiction of the whole family. Fathers and mothers were very involved in the day to day care of their children. Africans believed that caring for children is essential to the mental health of the child. The child's childhood experience is what will be passed down to the next generation (Billingsley, 1968).

For the duration of slavery parents were prohibited from caring for their children. The institution was created and implemented to dissolve the material and non-material elements of African culture. This would include caring for children. Africans have an expected way of caring for children that has roots in generations past. A child's emotional health was severely compromised during this time. The barriers set in place by the slave owner to prevent parents from caring for their children caused a lot of emotional trauma that negatively impacted the child's personality development; in addition, the experience between the mother and child was passed down to the next generation.

Children experienced broken bonds and no daily interaction with their parents (Dunaway, 2003). Slave owners controlled the rearing of slave children and family bonds were an obstacle to their primary goal, which was to create laborers as soon as possible that were entirely dependent on the master. On workdays, slave children received little or no supervision from their parents, who had to spend their entire workday in the fields or other plantation workplaces. Children were kept in plantation nurseries with their peers from other slave families, where they typically experienced malnutrition and injury due to poor supervision (Dunaway, 2003).

Such arrangements demolished the bond between slave parents and their children. Dunaway (2003) states,

> *"On the one hand, masters, not mothers, made fundamental decisions about the nature of child care: when, where, by whom, how much or how little. On the other hand, enslaved mothers did not have the option of not reporting to work when their children needed attention. Mothers risked punishment of children if they demanded better child care when the master's arrangements endangered their offspring. If the mother's caregiving conflicted with the master's work, she was required to do her "productive" work, most often in the fields or at the nonagricultural sites" (p. 69-70).*

Parents were forbidden to teach the child their native language, culture and dance. Parents were prohibited from protecting and comforting their children. Caring for children is an innate fundamental practice that has historical roots and is expected from the following generations, yet this group of people was prohibited from this experience. The observations Bowlby observed after birth between mother and child: a mother picking her child up; stroking her face with her fingertips; touching the head and body and putting the child to her breast was not allowed during this time. Mother and child were not allowed to bond through the natural caring a mother gives to her child. In addition, Bowlby believed a relaxed atmosphere, that provided enough time, is the best environment to nurture this type of preferred parenting to create a securely attached child. During slavery the atmosphere slaves experienced on a daily basis were an atmosphere filled with fear, uncertainty, physical punishment and a lot of loss. Far from the relaxed atmosphere suggested by Bowlby needed to develop a securely attached child. Mothers became unresponsive and did not want to give affection to their children due to knowing their fate. Mothers did not want to teach their children to obey the white slave owners and become good laborers for them. They did not want their children to be raised in an environment where they would be subject to the same cruel treatment. Many mothers wished their child was dead or had never been born (Donoghue, 2008). These feelings resulted in many women aborting their children and being very distant and emotionless with their children.

Influence of parents childhood experience

Consistent with the theory, the feelings a mother has toward her children is a direct reflection of her childhood experience. This is the transgenerational impact attachment has on the next generation. Mother's during slavery did not experience parenting from their parents and may not have experienced care from any adult. The parenting passed down to the children had to be fragmented. Parents were unable to respond to their children in times of distress therefore the child learned within himself how to react to stress and therefore if ever given an opportunity to parent would respond to their child in that manner. In the latter text an example was given of a child who has hurt himself and the way the parent responds is how the child will most likely respond in a similar situation in the future. I remember when I was a little girl my mom told me "I can't love you too much or get attached because I fear that something will happen if I do." I believe this is a behavior passed down from slavery because children were stripped from a mother's arm never to be seen again on a constant basis. Another memory I have growing up as a child is that no one said "I love you." My grandmother did not say it to my mother and my mother did not say it to me. I say it now to all my family members but many of them will not say it back. I believe this is another consequence of slavery because slaves were not allowed to have that emotion nor show the emotion to the people they cared about for fear that something would happen.

During slavery, children were left to care for themselves and therefore will most likely respond the same when they have children of their own.

The theory suggests that successful parenting requires parents to give a lot of their time and attention to develop a securely attached child. What we know about the history of slavery, children were often sold away from their parents; children were placed in plantation nurseries with countless amount of children with minimal supervision and parents were forced to work very long workdays and lived in different living quarters from their children (Henson, 2001).

Role of Attachment on Personality Development

Parents were not able to be an influence on the development of their child's personality throughout slavery. Slave owner's prohibited the care of the children by their parents. Slave Owner's took over that role. Mothers were not able to comfort and protect their children in times of distress. Children were not afforded an opportunity to learn from their parents how to respond in different situations. The lack of interaction from the mother during slavery developed an anxious avoidant attachment style for the child that would persist through their life span and be passed down to the next generation. This attachment style would impact their future relationships and for the purposes of this book, would greatly impact the romantic relationship between the man and the woman for generations.

Mending the Attachment through Couples Therapy

African Americans experienced an attachment rupture through the implementation of slavery that continues to impact the contemporary relationship. Emotionally Focused Therapy (EFT) also known as Emotionally Focused Couples Therapy (EFCT) can be used to rebuild the attachment within couples and address the historical attachment issues they experience.

> *"The goal of EFT is to reprocess experience and reorganize interactions to create a secure bond between the partners, a sense of secure connectedness. The focus here is always on attachment concerns; on safety, and contact; and on the obstacles to the above." (Johnson, 2004, p. 12).*

EFCT focuses on the process; the need for a safe, collaborative therapeutic alliance; there is a focus on emotion as the target and agent for change and finally a helpful emotional experience. The therapist works to find the destructive interaction patterns. "Unfolding key emotions and using them to prime new responses to one's partner in therapeutic enactments is the heart of change in EFT" (Johnson, 2004, p. 13). Attachment theory is used as a framework for thinking about relationships, Moreover, it is used specifically as a roadmap to understand adult intimacy. "Although this theory was first developed in the context of parent-child relationships it has now been applied to adult bonds. It outlines attachment needs for contact, comfort, security, and closeness as the features of this landscape" (Family Solutions Institute, 2009, p. 135).

EFCT was founded in the 1980s by Susan Johnson and Leslie Greenberg. Johnson was a clinical psychologist from Owatta, Canada, director of International Centre for Excellence in Emotionally Focused Therapy, director of the Ottawa Couple and Family Institute, and professor at the University of Ottawa and Alliant University in San Diego, California. Johnson and Greenberg believed people hid their "primary emotions" such as fear, loneliness, love or powerlessness etc. and instead communicated their "secondary emotions" defensiveness, disappointment and frustration etc. Communicating from the secondary emotions creates a self-perpetuating interactions that do not bring the couple closer nor does this interaction build more connectedness. The therapist attempts to create a safe atmosphere of protection so that the couples can be more vulnerable and comfortable to share their primary emotions. Secondary emotions are more reactive and create a negative interactional pattern. Communicate from their secondary emotions result in an insecure bond in the couple. Change occurs when the couple communicates with one another from their primary emotions, identify their primary emotional needs and create new patterns of interaction, thus creating a secure bond.

The historical attachment style inherited from slavery was an anxious avoidant attachment (insecure attachment). The secondary emotions experienced by this group defensiveness, disappointment and/or frustration are the negative interaction pattern that is consistent within this relationship. Primary emotions such as fear, hope, love loneliness, abandonment and powerlessness are emotions that African Americans were not allowed to express or verbalize. Slavery forced this group of people to stuff those types of emotions if they wanted to survive. Slaves were not able to express or feel any motions for another person; if the slave owner noticed this type of behavior a slave could be sold, beaten or killed. Helping the couple to speak from their primary emotions and see their partner in a more humanistic way will help build their attachment bond and build more connectedness.

The main focus of EFCT is working with individuals to be able to understand and give meaning to their emotions by looking at his or her primary and secondary emotions along with instrumental and maladaptive emotions. Primary emotions are the raw emotions that individuals feel based on the situation at hand (Greenberg, 2004; Greenberg & Goldman, 2008). The emotions can be but are not limited to happiness, sadness, anger, disappointment, and excitement. Secondary emotions are the emotions that individuals feel in response to their primary emotions (Greenberg, 2004; Greenberg & Goldman, 2008). For example, if an individual feels guilty or ashamed of himself and cannot create meaning for the emotion, an individual can become angry to mask the guilt or shame. Instrumental emotions are the emotions the person uses to influence or manipulate another person's thoughts and actions and can either be conscious or unconscious (Greenberg, 2004; Greenberg & Goldman, 2008). For instance, if a wife wants her husband to be more affectionate toward her but he does not make an effort to meet that need, then she may become angry to see if it can move him to be more affectionate. Maladaptive emotions are the emotions tied to trauma from the past that continue to surface, even though the individual is no longer in the traumatic setting (Greenberg, 2004; Greenberg & Goldman, 2008). The resurfacing is due to the unresolved trauma the person still carries. These emotions can include loneliness, worthlessness, shame, and abandonment (Greenberg, 2004; Greenberg & Goldman, 2008). Due to the historical trauma of this group many African Americans feel the above named emotions. These couples need to learn to feel safe enough to learn to share these primary emotions and explore where they came from. In addition they need to learn how to apply these relational skills to their relationship. Due to the structure of slavery men and women did not have an opportunity to develop these relational skills. Furthermore, due to institutional systematic racism these couples have not been afforded a long period of time to develop these relational skills.

There has been much empirical research done using EFCT in working with couples. The results are promising that EFCT works to develop a healthier attachment between the couple. There are certain populations where EFCT would not be the best theory to use such as couples who are ready to leave the relationship and individuals who are highly intellectual (Bevilacqua & Dattilio, 2000). EFCT requires the individual to be vulnerable and have the ability as well as being open to experiencing into their emotions. People who are more comfortable with reason and have difficulty with their emotions may not do well with this type of therapy. EFCT is a humanistic approach to therapy that recognizes the importance of emotion and emotional experiences. "Furthermore, EFT works to create new kinds of interactions within the couple system and to foster secure bonding between the partners" (Family Solutions Institute, 2009, p. 134).

Discussion

Additionally, therapeutic ideas informed by feminist theory should be explored to address gender-related power dynamics in heterosexual intimate African-American couples. Feminist theory can aid in helping the couple to be more flexible in the roles they carry-out in the relationship. More specifically, helping the couple to identify roles that will balance the power in the relationship. For example, what roles could the man take on in the relationship that would identify to the woman that he was able to protect and provide for their family?

Conclusion

The implementation of slavery and the process of breeding slaves, not only dismantled the family and its ability to socialize children and stabilize the adult personality. This process also created an attachment rupture that has not been able to mend to this day in the African American romantic relationship. An anxious avoidant attachment style was inherited by this group of people. EFCT is the recommended approach to address the attachment issues within the couple to create new interactions within the couple system and to foster secure bonding between the couple.

REFERENCES

Andrews, W. L.,& Gates, H. L. (2002). *Slave narratives*. New York: Library of America.

Bennett, L. (1969). *Before the Mayflower; a history of black America*. Chicago: Johnson Pub. Co.

Berman, W. H., & Sperling, M. B. (1994). The structure and function of adult attachment. In M.B. Berman, & W. H. Sperling (Eds), *Attachment in adults: clinical and developmental perspectives*. New York, London: Guilford.

Bevilacqua, L. & Dattilio, F.M. (2000). *Comparative Treatments for Relationship Dysfunction*. New York, NY: Springer Publishing Company.

Billingsley, A. (1968). *Black families in white America*. Englewood Cliffs, NJ: Prentice-Hall.

Black genealogy revisited: Restorying an African American family. (2008). In M. McGoldrick & K. V. Hardy (Eds.), *Re-visioning family therapy: Race, culture, and gender in clinical practice* (2nd ed.). New York, NY: Guilford.

Bowlby, J. (1969). *Attachment vol. 1*. New York, NY: Basic Books Inc., Publishers.

Bowlby, J. (1973). Attachment and loss: vol. 2: *Separation : Anxiety and anger*. London, NY: Tavistock Institute of Human Relations.

Bowlby, J. (1980). *Attachment and loss: vol. 3: Loss: sadness and depression*. London, NY: Tavistock Institute of Human Relations.

Bowlby, J. (1988). *John Bowlby A secure base: Clinical applications of attachment theory*. London, NY: Routledge Classics.

Carson, E. A. (2014). Prisoners in 2014. *U.S. department of justice office of justice programs bureau justice statistician*.

Collins, D. (1971). *Practical rules for the management and medical treatment of negro Slaves in the sugar colonies*. New York: Books for Libraries Press.

De Las Casas, B., & Phillips, J. (1656). *The tears of the indians.* New York, NY: Knopf.

Day, J. C., & Newburger, E. C. (2002). *The big payoff: Educational attainment and synthetic estimates of work-life earnings.* Washington, DC: U.S. Census Bureau, U.S. Department of Commerce, Economics and Statistics Administration.

Donoghue, E. (2008). *Black breeding machines: The breeding of Negro slaves in the diaspora.* Bloomington, IN: Authorhouse.

Dunaway, W. A. (2003). *The African-American family in slavery and emancipation.* New York, NY: Maison des Sciences de l'homme/ Cambridge University Press.

Family Solutions Institute. (2009). *Preparation workshop for the marriage & family therapy national licensing exam.* Jamaica Plain, MA: The Family Solutions Corporation.

Fogel, R. W. & Engerman, S. L. (1974). *Time on the cross: the economics of american negro slavery.* Boston and Torontof: Little, Brown and Company.

Fortes, M. (2008). *Kinship and marriage among the Ashanti.*

Gertrude Clarke Whittall Poetry and Literature Fund, Ellison, R., & Shapiro, K. (1964). *The writer's experience.* Washington, DC: Published for the Library of Congress by theGertrude Clarke Whittall Poetry and Literature Fund; [for sale by the Superintendent ofDocuments, U.S. Govt. Print. Off.

Graff, G. (2014). The Intergenerational Trauma of Slavery and its Aftermath, *The Journal of Psychohistory 41* (3) Winter, pp. 181-197

Greenberg, L.S. (2004). Emotion-focused Therapy. *Clinical Psychology and Psychotherapy, vol 11,* 3-16.

Greenberg, L.S & Goldman, R.N. (2008) *Emotion-Focused Couples Therapy: The Dynamics ofEmotion, Love, and Power.* Washington, DC: American Psychological Association.

Henson, J. (2001). *The life of Josiah Henson: Formerly a slave, now an inhabitant of Canada.* Bedford, MA: Applewood Books.

Johnson, S. (2004). *The practice of emotionally focused couple therapy* (2nd ed.). New York:Brunner-Routledge.

Kaufman, P., Alt, M. N., & Chapman, C. D. (n.d.). Dropout Rates in the United States: 2001.

Kurth, W. (2013). Attachment theory and psychohistory. *The Journal of Psychohistory*, *41*(2). Leach, M. T., & Williams, S. A. (2007). The Impact of the Academic achievement Gap on the African American Family. *Journal of Human Behavior in the Social Environment*, *15*(2-3), 39-59.

Marris, P. (1991). The social construction of uncertainty. In C. M. Parkes (Ed.), J. Stevenson-Hilde (Ed.), *Attachment across the life cycle. (pp. 77-90).* London, New York:Routledge

Morrow, A. (2003). *Breaking the curse of willie lynch: the science of slave psychology.*

Parsons, T., & Bales, R. F. (1955). *Family, socialization and interaction process.* Glencoe, IL: Free Press.

Swenson, D. (2004). *A neo-functionalist synthesis of theories in family sociology.*Lewiston, NY: Edwin Mellen Press.

Treas, J., & Giesen, D. (2000). Sexual Infidelity Among Married and Cohabiting Americans.
Journal of Marriage and Family, 62(1), 48-60.

Vespa, J., Lewis, J. M., & Kreider, R. M. (2013). America's families and living arrangements: 2012 population characteristics. *United States Census Bureau*, (August 2013), P20-570.

About the Author

Sametta E. Hill lives in Minneapolis, MN with her family. She holds a doctoral degree from Argosy University in Marriage and Family Therapy. She has worked in the Department of Human Services for over 14 years, serving children, adolescents, adults and families in the areas of economic assistance, child protection and juvenile corrections. She has an article published in the Psychohistory News titled *Psychic Slavery and Trust in African American Intimate Relationships*. She is the author of *Ruptured Attachment,* The historical problem within African American intimate relationships and why it affects us today. Her passion is to bring awareness to the historical pain that African Americans continue to embody and to help African Americans heal from hurts experienced throughout history that continue to affect the family bond and structure.

CPSIA information can be obtained
at www.ICGtesting.com
Printed in the USA
FSHW011141230420
69481FS